17.49   3/25/13

W9-BQZ-388

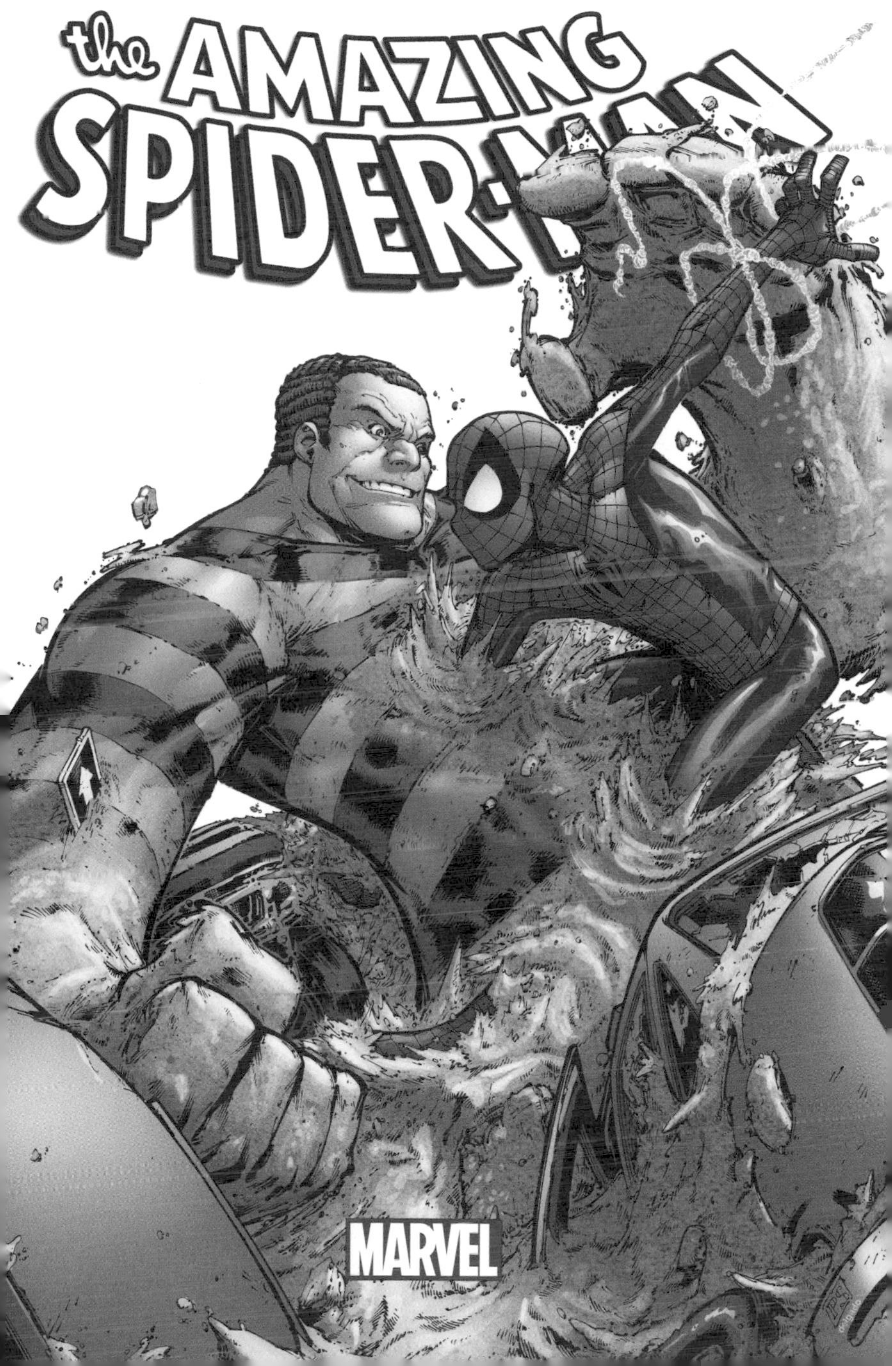
the AMAZING SPIDER-MAN
MARVEL

AMAZING SPIDER-MAN VOL. 4: THE SANDMAN YOUNG READERS NOVEL. First printing 2012. ISBN# 978-0-7851-6613-9. Published by MARVEL WORLDWIDE, INC., a subsidiary of MARVEL ENTERTAINMENT, LLC. OFFICE OF PUBLICATION: 135 West 50th Street, New York, NY 10020. Copyright © 2012 Marvel Characters, Inc. All rights reserved. $6.99 per copy in the U.S. and $7.99 in Canada (GST #R127032852); Canadian Agreement #40668537. All characters featured in this issue and the distinctive names and likenesses thereof, and all related indicia are trademarks of Marvel Characters, Inc. No similarity between any of the names, characters, persons, and/or institutions in this magazine with those of any living or dead person or institution is intended, and any such similarity which may exist is purely coincidental. **Printed in the U.S.A.** ALAN FINE, EVP - Office of the President, Marvel Worldwide, Inc. and EVP & CMO Marvel Characters B.V.; DAN BUCKLEY, Publisher & President - Print, Animation & Digital Divisions; JOE QUESADA, Chief Creative Officer; TOM BREVOORT, SVP of Publishing; DAVID BOGART, SVP of Operations & Procurement, Publishing; RUWAN JAYATILLEKE, SVP & Associate Publisher, Publishing; C.B. CEBULSKI, SVP of Creator & Content Development; DAVID GABRIEL, SVP of Publishing Sales & Circulation; MICHAEL PASCIULLO, SVP of Brand Planning & Communications; JIM O'KEEFE, VP of Operations & Logistics; DAN CARR, Executive Director of Publishing Technology; SUSAN CRESPI, Editorial Operations Manager; ALEX MORALES, Publishing Operations Manager; STAN LEE, Chairman Emeritus. For information regarding advertising in Marvel Comics or on Marvel.com, please contact Niza Disla, Director of Marvel Partnerships, at ndisla@marvel.com. For Marvel subscription inquiries, please call 800-217-9158. **Manufactured between 8/27/2012 and 10/1/2012 by SHERIDAN BOOKS, INC., CHELSEA, MI, USA.**

10 9 8 7 6 5 4 3 2 1

THE SANDMAN

Writer
JOE CARAMAGNA
Comic Artist
SCOTT KOBLISH
Colorist
SOTOCOLOR
Letterer
JOE CARAMAGNA
Cover Artists
PATRICK SCHERBERGER with EDGAR DELGADO
Spot Illustrations
SCOTT KOBLISH with SOTOCOLOR
and PAUL RYAN, JOHN ROMITA & DAMION SCOTT
Comic Editor
JORDAN D. WHITE
Prose Editor
CORY LEVINE

Assistant Editors: Alex Starbuck & Nelson Ribeiro
Editors, Special Projects: Jennifer Grünwald & Mark D. Beazley
Senior Editor, Special Projects: Jeff Youngquist
Senior Vice President of Sales: David Gabriel
Associate Publisher & SVP of Print, Animation and Digital Media: Ruwan Jayatilleke
SVP of Brand Planning & Communications: Michael Pasciullo
Book Design: Marie Drion & Joe Frontirre

Editor In Chief: Axel Alonso
Chief Creative Officer: Joe Quesada
Publisher: Dan Buckley
Executive Producer: Alan Fine

SPIDER-MAN

The former professional wrestler turned super hero learned the hard way that with great power must come great responsibility. To make up for his past mistakes, he has vowed to protect New York City from all those who wish to do harm.

PETER PARKER

Raised from childhood by his Uncle Ben and Aunt May, he always dreamed of becoming a scientist like his late father. But after a lab accident — and a radioactive spider bite — granted him special powers, he discovered his true calling.

UNCLE BEN

As Peter's father figure, Uncle Ben has taught him many life lessons. But the most important one of all is that "with great power there must also come great responsibility."

AUNT MAY

After the death of Peter's parents, May Parker and her husband, Ben, raised their nephew as if he was their own child.

FLASH THOMPSON

Eugene "Flash" Thompson is Midtown High's star football player but also its biggest bully. Little does he know his favorite victim, Peter Parker, is really New York City's greatest super hero!

J. JONAH JAMESON

The publisher of *The Daily Bugle* brings attention to his floundering newspaper by going after New York City's beloved costumed vigilante.

CAPTAIN STACY

A veteran of the police department, Captain Stacy keeps law and order in New York City.

THE VULTURE

Adrian Toomes spent his life as an engineer but never felt appreciated by his employers. After he was fired, he decided to use his greatest invention, the Vulture harness, to gain the respect he felt he always deserved.

SANDMAN

While on the run from the police, a chemical accident left criminal Flint Marko with the ability to turn his body into sand.

DOCTOR OCTOPUS

Dr. Otto Octavius is a world-renowned, yet accident-prone, nuclear physicist. After one accident too many left him melded to a set of four mechanical arms, he became Spider-Man's most formidable super villain!

GREEN GOBLIN

Norman Osborn is a military contractor who was tasked with developing a super-soldier serum. But aside from extraordinary abilities, his flawed formula also brings out his devilish dark side!

KRAVEN THE HUNTER

After conquering the fiercest animals in all the jungles of Africa, the hunter Sergei Kravinoff set his sights on the most elusive game of them all: the Amazing Spider-Man!

THE LIZARD

Dr. Curt Connors developed a serum to replicate a lizard's ability to regenerate limbs in humans. But when he tested it on himself, he got more than he bargained for!

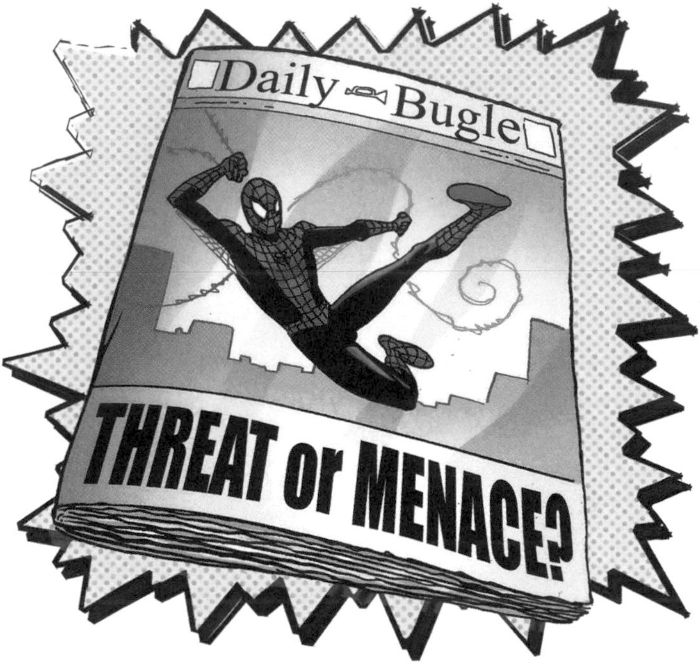

Daily Bugle
THREAT or MENACE?

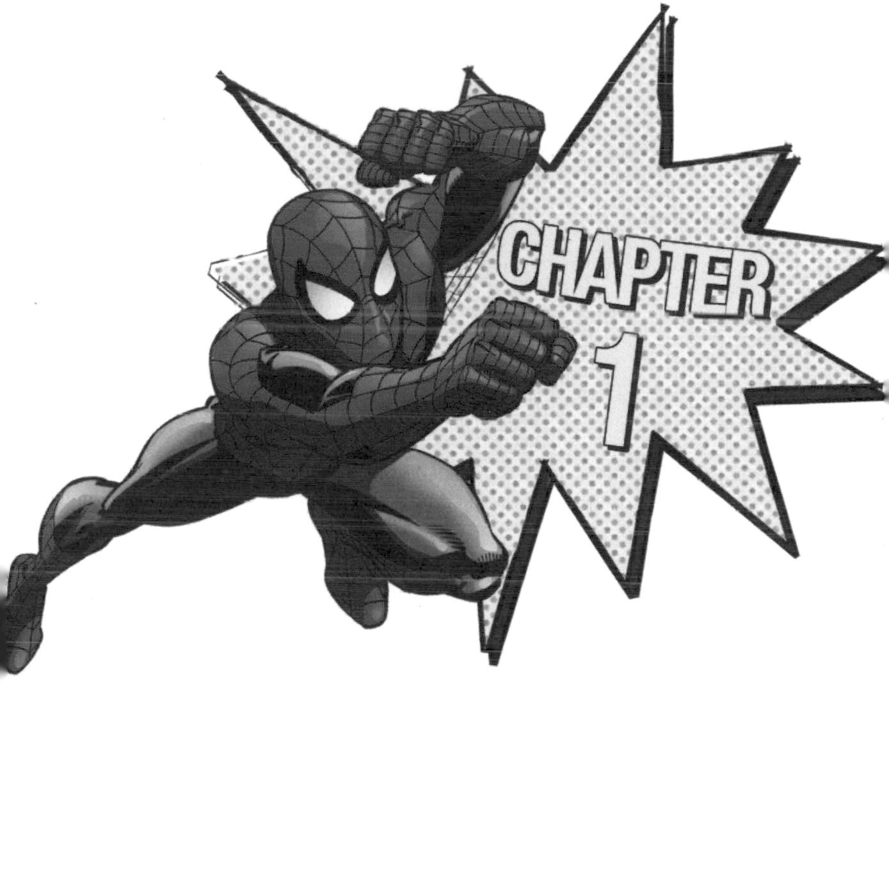
CHAPTER
1

The nightmare is always the same. While attending a lecture on radiology during a class trip, Midtown High student Peter Parker is bitten by a radioactive spider. When he leaves the lab, he discovers the spider somehow transferred its proportional abilities to him — and now Peter has superhuman strength, speed, agility and the power to stick to walls! At first, Peter uses his powers to cash in and become the superstar professional wrestler

known only as the Amazing Spider-Man! But one evening after a match, Spider-Man sees a robbery in progress. Although he has the power to stop it, he chooses to let the criminal get away. Late that night when he returns home, he discovers the man who raised him from childhood, his dear Uncle Ben, has been shot and killed by a burglar. Seeking revenge, Peter puts on his Spider-Man costume and corners the burglar in an abandoned warehouse. When he captures his uncle's killer, he realizes it's the same criminal he had the chance to stop earlier. Through the immeasurable heartache of losing his Uncle Ben, Peter learns that with his great power comes great responsibility — and Spider-Man becomes New York City's newest super hero!

The problem is, it isn't a dream. This is Peter Parker's life. While most boys dream of becoming astronauts or playing for the New York Mets, all Peter sees anymore when he closes his eyes to go to sleep are these memories that play in his mind like the same movie every single night.

"Parker!

"Peter Parker!"

The shrill voice echoed in Peter's head, startling him so he jumped right out of his chair, sending his schoolbooks flying.

"Ah! Get back, it's Doctor Octopus!" Peter screamed as he hit the floor. Realizing where he was, he didn't need to look up at Ms. Pranfree's icy gaze to know what had happened. The laughter of his classmates told him

he'd done it again. He'd fallen asleep in class.

Patrolling New York City's streets as the Amazing Spider-Man late at night for the past few weeks was taking its toll on Peter. He had become very forgetful, missed a lot of homework assignments and was regularly falling asleep in class. In the past, Aunt May would have grounded him for letting his school grades slip. But ever since Uncle Ben had passed away, Peter had become a master at hiding things from her — not just because he felt guilty for what had happened to his uncle, but because he didn't want to risk Aunt May finding out his super-hero identity. It was easiest just to avoid her. He even lied and told her he got a job at a restaurant so he had an excuse to spend more time out of the house.

Peter rubbed his eyes awake and felt the sting of the purple-and-blue ring that had grown around his left eye — a reminder of his last encounter with a freaky super villain.

"Mr. Rodriguez wants to see you in his office right away, Peter."

Peter scooped up the pile of books that had fallen to the floor and stuffed them into his backpack as his classmates snickered. The loudest laughter, of course, was Flash Thompson's. It was the unmistakable evil chuckle he had heard every day since they were six years old — when Flash gave him the nickname "Puny

Parker" on the school playground. Back then, Peter had wished someday he would be strong enough to stop Flash from ever bullying him again. He had wished it when they were nine years old, and Flash had shoved him into a patch of poison oak on their Boy Scout camping trip. He had wished it when they were 12, and Flash had filled his backpack with dirt at recess. He had wished it when they were 14, and Flash had stolen Peter's underpants from his gym locker and hung them from the flagpole for the whole school to see. The pair with the purple dinosaurs on them.

When Peter had been bitten by the radioactive spider and gotten his incredible powers, he had thought he would finally get payback. But he couldn't let Flash know his secret. If his cover was blown, all Peter's friends and family would be in danger from Spider-Man's enemies. Not to mention all the trouble he'd get into from *Daily Bugle* Publisher J. Jonah Jameson, who was paying Peter for photos of Spider-Man.

As he turned toward the door with his backpack slung over his shoulder, a wet, squishy spitball flew at him from across the room and splashed down on Peter's right temple!

"Are you finally gonna fess up, chicken? Cluck! Cluck!" Flash said, flapping his elbows up and down.

"Ah, Peter! Nice to see you! Sit down, pal." Mr. Rodriguez leaned back in his chair with his feet up on his desk and repeatedly bounced a rubber ball against a nearby wall with a KA-THUNK, KA-THUNK, KA-THUNK. Peter was already annoyed by the way he had been greeted, as though he had shown up unannounced and caught Mr. Rodriguez off-guard during some downtime. That kind of thing might have seemed cool to other students, but Peter hated it.

Mr. Rodriguez was Midtown High's football, basketball and baseball coach.

and a pretty good one at that. Midtown High had won city championships in all three sports during the past two years thanks to him — and a certain star athlete named Flash Thompson. Because those were all after-school activities, Peter suspected Principal Conway had to give Mr. Rodriguez something to do during school hours to justify his coaching jobs, so he had given him the job that required the least amount of work: guidance counselor. But as long as Peter had known him, had been counseling was limited to the one time when he had shown Peter how to rock the vending machines back and forth when his granola bar had gotten got stuck last spring. It was the only time Mr. Rodriguez had paid any attention to Peter at all.

If you looked down the hall any

given day, you might see Mr. Rodriguez holding court with his athletes, recounting stories of his college-football glory days, or with a group of teachers, trying to recruit them for his weekly game of poker. Peter thought of him as a future version of Flash Thompson — which is exactly why Peter didn't like him.

He had no idea why Mr. Rodriguez would want to see him. That is, until he spotted an open copy of *The Daily Bugle* on his desk.

"There's something I'd like to talk to you about." KA-THUNK! went the rubber ball against the wall.

"I *know* what you want to talk about, and it's not true," Peter interrupted.

"Pardon?" said Mr. Rodriguez, catching the ball in his hand.

"What happened with Sandman. I

know what people are saying about me, and it's not true."

"Oh, right. *Sandman,*" Mr. Rodriguez said. Peter hated to be patronized. Of course he knew what Peter was talking about — the newspaper with the Sandman's face on the front page was right there on the desk under his elbow! "Well, if you feel there's more to the story, now's your chance to set things straight. That's what I'm here for. To listen."

The last thing Peter wanted to do was talk to Mr. Rodriguez about it, but he was right. This was his chance to tell his side of the story. Peter spent his nights running toward danger as Spider-Man — not away from it — and he was going to make sure they knew he was much braver than they thought. So Peter started to tell Mr. Rodriguez exactly what had happened.

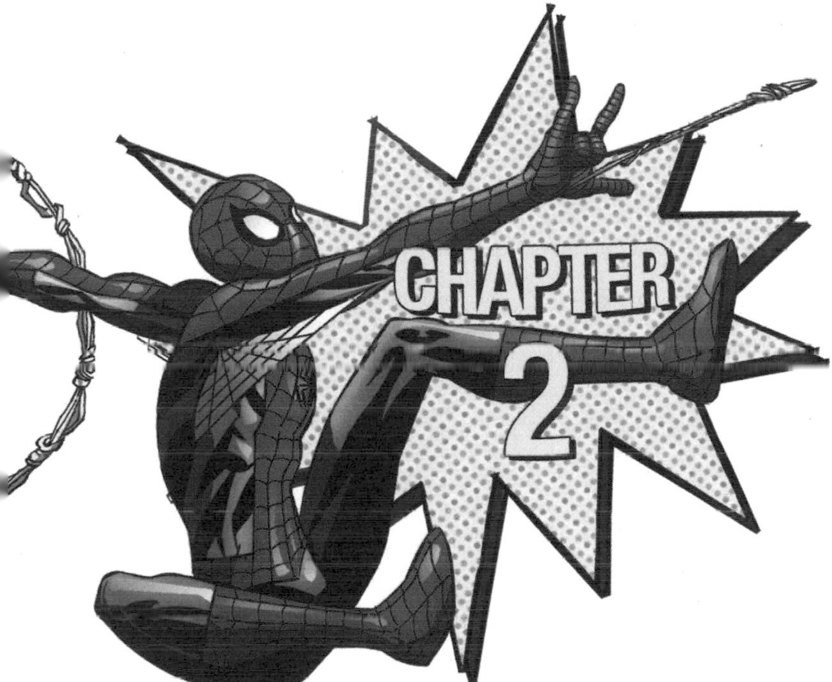
CHAPTER
2

It all began in Ms. Pranfree's fifth period physics class.

Peter Parker used to wonder about certain students at Midtown High — the underachievers who showed up late for class and then slept through the whole thing. What was so hard about finishing your homework, studying and making it through a day without getting detention? But during the past few weeks, he had become one of them. His late nights were catching up with him. There he was, sleeping through Ms. Pranfree's lecture on the different forms of energy.

"So energy can't be created or destroyed, it just changes form," she said, scribbling scientific formulas on the chalkboard. "For example, light from the sun shines on the snow, causing the snow's molecules to move faster until the snow melts into water.

The sunlight starts as light energy and becomes thermal energy. Heat."

Peter snored at his desk. Ms. Pranfree continued, "Chemical energy, mechanical energy — like light, they can *all* become thermal energy, including electrical energy. That's why lightning is the leading cause of forest fires."

Ms. Pranfree stepped in front of a large machine standing at the head of the class. To the students, it looked like a mad scientist's secret weapon from an old science fiction movie with its tall, cylindrical body and a spinning saucer for a head. Two cords that looked like the ends of a jump rope came out of the machine's sides, with small metal contacts at the ends of the handles. Ms. Pranfree flipped a switch on the machine and took a cord handle in each hand as it hummed to life.

"Lightning strikes when the negative charges in a storm cloud are attracted to the positive charges on the ground below. This StarkTech generator can simulate those conditions by sucking in air and bouncing its particles off each other. The energy it generates will separate into positive and negative charges. When I hold these contacts close together, the negative charge from one end will attract the positive charge on the other and create a lightning strike between them!"

Normally, Peter would have found this kind of lecture fascinating, but he could barely keep his eyes open and drifted to sleep at his desk.

"Then it will measure the amount of light energy, thermal energy and sound energy the lightning generates. The longer the particles bounce off each other, the stronger the charge — so handle this equipment very carefully."

Peter would later tell Mr. Rodriguez it was the sudden slam of the door that shook him awake from his nap, but that wasn't the whole truth. It was the alarm bells of his spider-sense ringing in his ears that woke him up, warning him there was danger nearby. Peter had gotten used to his internal early warning system when it tingled in his brain while out on the streets or swinging between buildings at night, but he was always safe at school. As long as Flash Thompson was out of arm's reach, there was never any danger to worry about.

A big, burly ox of a man in a striped sweater lumbered into the classroom. He was so tall he had to duck to keep from bumping his tightly cropped head on his way through the door. But there were a lot of tough guys living in New York — that alone shouldn't have been enough to set off Peter's spider-sense. Judging by his smile, the man looked pleasant enough, and he certainly seemed excited to see Ms. Pranfree. The only thing indicating this man might be dangerous was Ms. Pranfree's reaction. With the machine still running, she dropped the lightning contacts to the floor and covered her open mouth with her fingers.

"F-Flint?" Ms. Pranfree said, taking two steps backwards.

"Eliza!" He threw his arms out to open himself up for a hug that didn't come.

"Flint...y-you're out?"

"I *escaped*," Flint said.

"You *what? How?*"

Peter started to worry. As the man she called "Flint" walked closer to her, Ms. Pranfree slowly backed away, not letting him get too close. He obviously didn't get the hint. As he kept advancing toward her, his smile stretched from ear to ear.

"Eliza, something amazing's happened. Do you remember when I was on the run? How the cops caught up to me at the beach and smoked me out of that cave? There was some chemical waste in there. Biohazard stuff! When they tossed their canisters of tear gas at me, they must have mixed together and caused a chemical reaction and...well, in the months after they locked me up, I felt my body changing. I'm different. Not human anymore."

An escaped convict? Peter thought. He looked around the room for a place to change into his Spider-Man costume without being seen —

another detail he couldn't share with Mr. Rodriguez — and saw the rest of his classmates gripping the corners of their desks, petrified of the stranger.

Flint backed her all the way to the window until she was cornered with nowhere to go. "Your body? Changing?" she said. "Not human?"

When they heard the sound of the police sirens approaching the school, screaming through the air, the students didn't feel any safer. It made them more nervous about what was going to happen. Nobody knew what to do, and Peter's spider-sense was rocking his brain. His forehead started to sweat.

"I'll explain it to you later," Flint said, pulling at Ms. Pranfree's shoulders. "We don't have much time. We gotta go."

"Flint, you're scaring me," she said,

pushing his hands away. "I'm not going anywhere with you. After what you've done..."

Flint grabbed her shoulders again, but this time his gentle touch was replaced by an angry grip. Her flesh turned white under his thick fingers. The veins in his neck bulged. "After what I've done?" he shouted. "I did it all for you!"

"Freeze, Marko!" Officers Slott and Ramos burst through the door and fixed their guns on him. Flint Marko marched right for the officers, barely noticing their weapons. "What will you do to me? Do you think you can send me back to jail?"

As Flint barreled toward the two officers, Peter noticed something strange happening to him. His once-smooth cheeks and chin grew coarse — as if Flint was aging right before his eyes! With each step he took toward the police officers, his big hands grew even larger and rougher. And when Flint blinked, Peter swore his eyelashes kicked up a flutter of dust. A fine powder billowed from all over his body. No, it wasn't powder — it was sand! The officers backed away, careful not to make any sudden movements to provoke him, but the man moving toward them was no longer Flint

Marko. He was a hulking, rage-filled SAND MONSTER!

Marko raised his left hand, which had grown to the size of a boulder. As he tightened his fingers into a fist, it took the shape of a large hammer. The tighter he clenched, the denser it became until it was like a block of concrete. His other hand exploded from his arm like a geyser of sand and knocked Officer Ramos off his feet. The giant hammer that was once Marko's left hand clubbed Officer Slott to the floor. In the chaos, Peter saw his opportunity.

Marko stood over the fallen officers and held his arms out over them. Sand flowed from them like a waterfall, filling their mouths, noses, ears and eyes. "Believe me, there's no cell that will ever hold a man made out of sand!" he laughed as they struggled to breathe.

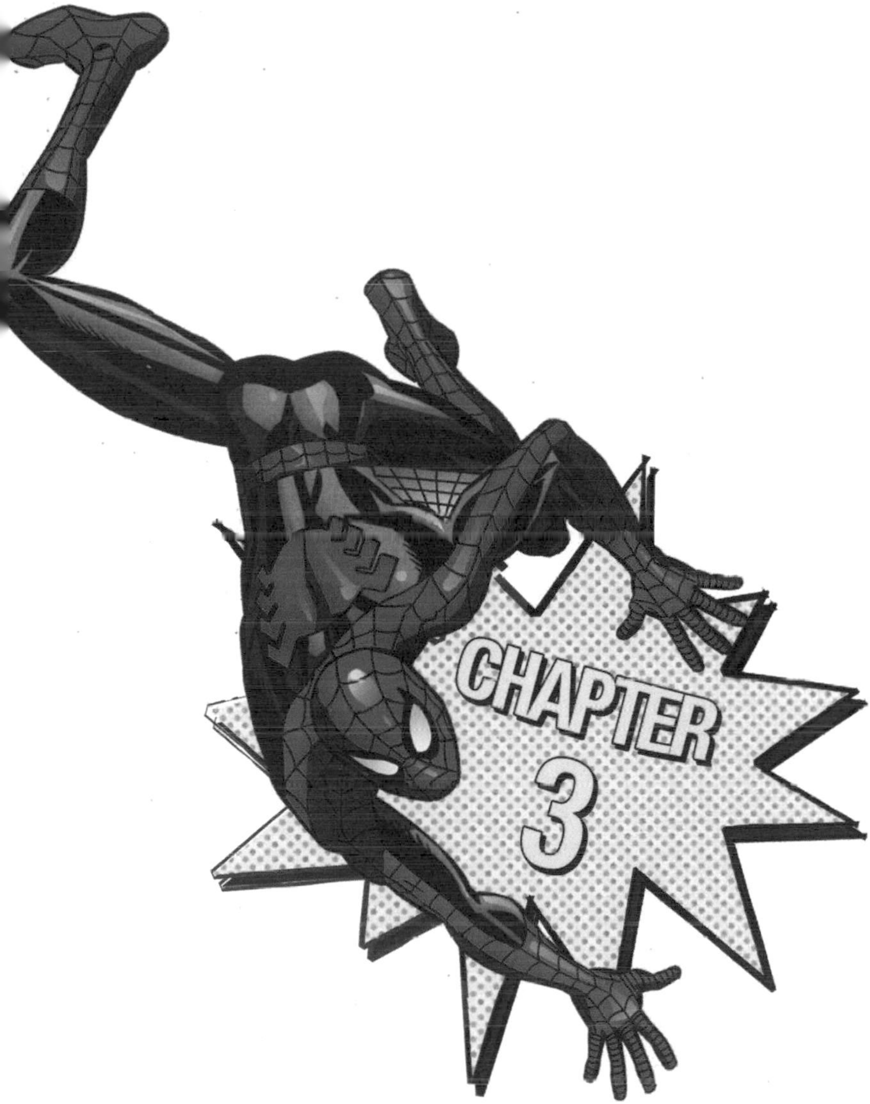
CHAPTER
3

Mr. Rodriguez wasn't buying it.

"And you saw this? With your own eyes?"

"Yes," Peter insisted.

"So what happened next?"

Peter looked down at the floor. He couldn't tell Mr. Rodriguez what had happened next, because Peter Parker wasn't there for it...only Spider-Man was. And he didn't want *anyone* to know he was Spider-Man, let alone Mr. Rodriguez.

The guidance counselor shook his head and turned his attention back to the wall, bouncing his rubber ball again. KA-THUNK! KA-THUNK! KA-THUNK! "I guess he was right."

"What?" Peter asked.

"That's not the story I heard."

"What did *you* hear?"

KA-THUNK! Mr. Rodriguez caught the ball in his hand and held it this time. "This guy, Flint Marko, busted into your physics class, right? He grabbed Ms. Pranfree and threw her over his shoulder. But when he tried to get away, Officer Slott and Officer Ramos blocked the door."

"Well, that's not exactly..." Peter started to say.

"The cops took a couple shots at him, BLAM! BLAM!" Mr. Rodriguez closed one eye and waved finger guns in the air. *Just in case the two-time science-fair winner doesn't know what guns look like?* Peter thought.

"But the bullets...he swallowed them up into his sandy chest, and then spit them out on the floor," Mr. Rodriguez continued. "The cops tried to run, but Marko chased them. His hands grew, like huge, and he knocked them out with one punch each. POW! POW! And then he said some crazy thing like, 'You can call me Sandman! Obey the Sandman!' And that's when Flash Thompson took control of the situation."

"Flash Thompson?!" Peter stood up out of his chair, but Mr. Rodriguez motioned for him to sit back down.

"Easy. I'm just telling you what I heard from your classmate," Mr. Rodriguez said. "Flash flipped over a bunch of desks and yelled for everyone to duck down behind them and crawl out in an orderly fashion. He put himself in harm's way to keep his classmates safe." Peter just shook his head.

"But he says when he started for the back door of the class, he saw you, backpack over your shoulder, pushing your classmates out of the way to get to safety." Mr. Rodriguez fixed his eyes on Peter's as he spoke, but Peter looked down at his shoes. "He called for you to help him get your friends out, but you were gone just like that. You didn't even turn around." Mr. Rodriguez kept his gaze fixed on Peter, expecting him to interrupt his version of the story and tell him it wasn't true, or that he had a reason for doing what he did. But he was met with silence. Of course Peter had a reason. A good reason — he had to change into Spider-Man, and he had

to do it far away from the rest of the class to keep his identity secret. But, of course, he couldn't tell Mr. Rodriguez the truth.

"So Flash lined up all the students and herded them out the door, one by one. The Sandman guy was pouring sand down the two cops' throats — I mean, really drowning them in sand — while Ms. Pranfree begged him to stop before he killed them. Suddenly, Spider-Man smashed through the window!

"Spidey looked over at Flash and said to him, 'Great job, buddy! You can be my official sidekick. Be my B.F.F., bro!' Then he launched himself at the Sandman and put a boot in the middle of his back, kicking up a whole lot of dust everywhere. Poof! Sandman was caught off-guard, so his body caved in like a giant sandcastle. He re-formed himself and turned around to see what had hit him, and Spidey got him good with a left cross. BAM! POW!"

When Mr. Rodriguez stood up and started shadowboxing behind his desk, Peter officially ran out of patience. "B.F.F.?!" he shouted.

Mr. Rodriguez dropped his boxing stance. "Yeah, it means 'best friend forever.'"

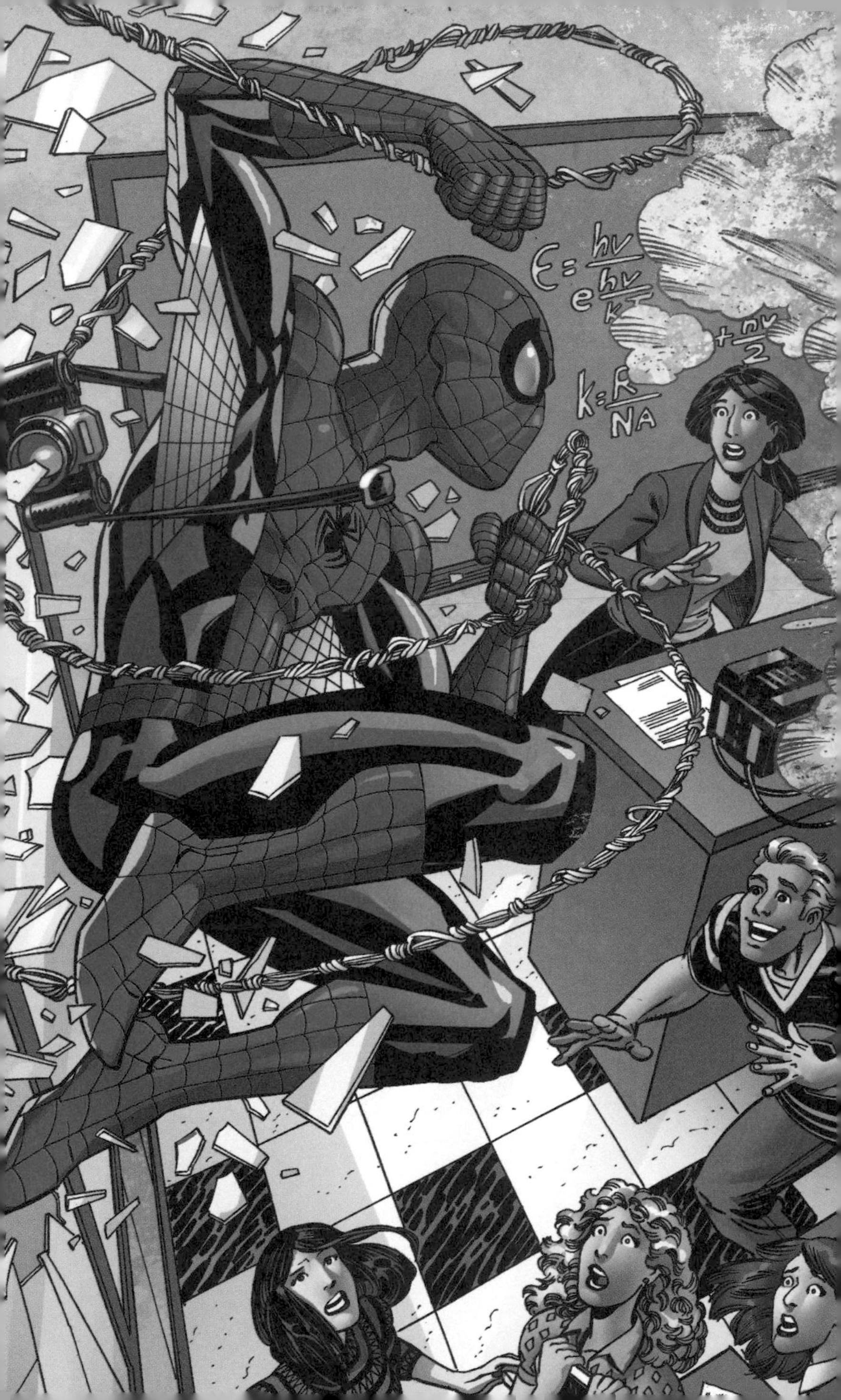

E = hv / e^(hv/kT)
+ hv/2
K = R / NA

"I know that!" Peter said. "But you don't have to be a genius to figure out who gave you this version of the story! Do you honestly believe this?"

Mr. Rodriguez leaned back in his chair and smiled. "Flash may have exaggerated a few of the details," he admitted. "But he said you pushed past everyone to get to the door. And I believe him. You were gone before Spider-Man ever got there, weren't you?"

Peter looked down again. He rubbed his face nervously and was reminded of the lingering purple-and-black bruise around his left eye. Of course Peter had been there. He had run out of the room only so he could come back in as his super-hero alter ego and take Sandman down. But he couldn't let Flash convince everyone he was a coward. He had to tell the rest of the story.

"I was there the whole time, Mr. Rodriguez. I saw everything. Flash is...we just don't get along," he put it mildly. "He wants everyone to think I'm scared. But I was there, and I can prove it"

"Okay, then. I'm listening. Tell me what *really* happened."

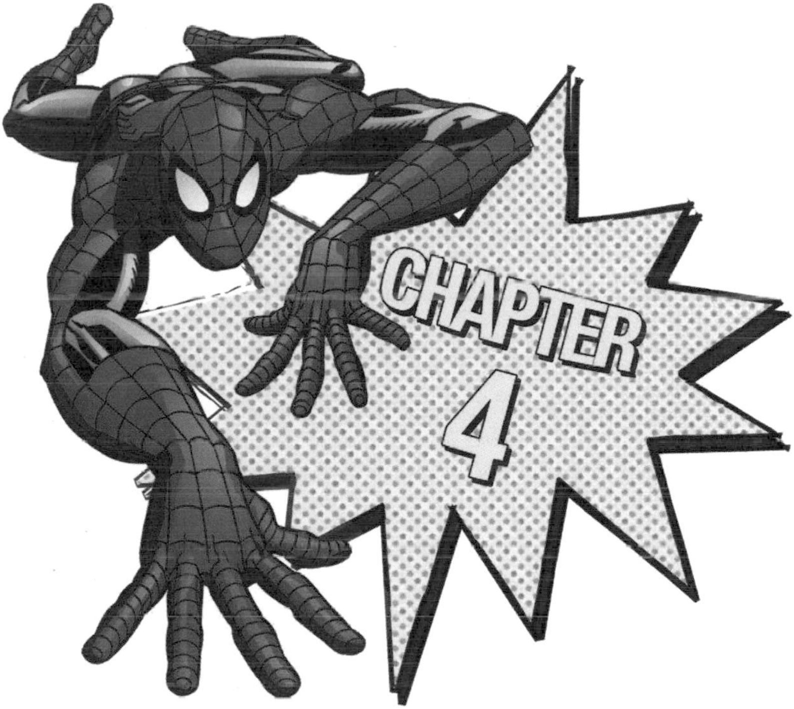
CHAPTER
4

Peter remembered it clearly: He had run out of the classroom and into the closest boys' restroom. Luckily, it was empty. He quickly changed into his Spider-Man costume and threw his school clothes into his backpack, where he saw Uncle Ben's camera. It had been a while since he sold any pictures to *The Daily Bugle*. But if he could get some photos of the Sandman, the money would help Aunt May get out of trouble.

Thanks to the efforts of Publisher J. Jonah Jameson, *The Daily Bugle* had become a hot seller because of its anti-Spider-Man stories. Spidey haters and Spidey lovers alike bought every issue just to see what the newspaper would say next about the wall-crawler. But Jameson didn't know his front-page pictures of Spider-Man were actually taken by Spider-Man himself!

Peter Parker used the self-timer on Uncle Ben's old camera to photograph himself in web-slinging action and hoped Jameson wouldn't have any choice but to print the truth. He was wrong. But the *Bugle* paid him  well for his photos, and he had to help Aunt May pay the rent with Uncle Ben gone. Because he didn't want Aunt May to worry about him chasing Spider-Man around the city — or worse, find out he *was* Spider-Man — Peter had made up a cover story about working as a dishwasher in a restaurant after school so she wouldn't ever learn his secret.

Peter grabbed the camera and stashed the rest of his stuff in a locked bathroom stall.

When Spider-Man crashed through
the window, Sandman was dousing
Officers Slott and Ramos with an
endless flow of sand coming out of his
arms like a faucet. Spider-Man kicked
him in the back, and the sandy man-
castle collapsed inside of himself!
That's it, Spider-Man thought. *He
doesn't* create *sand. His body transforms
into sand he controls by mental command,
the way a person's arms and legs move*

because the brain tells them to. The sand is coming from inside his body, leaving him hollow. Vulnerable.

When Sandman turned to see what had hit him, Spider-Man nailed him with a left cross on the chin that sent him hurtling into the hallway.

"Are you all right?" Spider-Man asked Ms. Pranfree, who nodded. "Good. Help these two officers and the rest of your students get to safety. I'll handle Marko."

"Go, Spider-Man, go!" Flash Thompson cheered.

When Spider-Man followed Sandman into the hallway, he was

already pulling his granules together
and getting back on his feet. Before
Spider-Man could web the camera to
the wall above the row of lockers, his
spider-sense tingled, ringing loudly in
his head.

Suddenly, an enormous
sledgehammer made of sand crashed
into the lockers with incredible force.
Thanks to the early warning of his
spider-sense, Spider-Man leaped out
of the way just in time. A moment
later he would have been smashed to

bits! But his camera wasn't so lucky, as the Sandman's mighty blow sent it crashing to the floor.

Again and again, Sandman swung his mighty arms, their sand formed into dense blocks, but each time Spider-Man flipped and flopped and tumbled and tossed himself out of harm's way. "You're just as slippery as they say," Sandman grumbled through clenched teeth. But as

Spidey dodged the hits, he put more distance between himself and Uncle Ben's camera. Without the pictures to sell to *The Bugle*, he and Aunt May would be evicted from their apartment for sure!

"Don't worry, Spidey, I got it!" a voice called out from behind the smashed metal lockers lying on the floor. Spider-Man saw Flash Thompson run out into the hall from Ms. Pranfree's classroom to pick up the camera!

"Flash, get back inside!" Ms. Pranfree tried to grab him by the shirt, but he was already gone.

"What?! Flash...er, kid...listen to your teacher!" Spidey said. But Flash put the camera up to his face and snapped pictures of the Sandman as he missed punch after sandy punch. But the blows came so quickly Spider-Man was on the defensive and couldn't get a chance to strike back. Spider Man knew eventually one of those punches was going to make contact. Not only would he get hurt if he didn't turn the fight in his favor soon, but so could Ms. Pranfree and Flash!

Spider-Man jumped from one wall of lockers to the other. With a quick jab, he broke the glass over the fire alarm. The bells rang loudly. In an instant, the sprinklers on the ceiling squeaked to life and rained water down on all of them.

Sandman looked down as water soaked his body. His sandy skin turned dark with moisture, and his arms grew heavy. His softening facial features started to run. "No," he muttered. Within seconds, the weight of his heavy, wet sand was pulling him down. His once-powerful legs disappeared into a heap of mud on the floor. His body collapsed in on itself until he lost shape up to his chest. "No!" He shouted this time — until finally his shoulders, neck, mouth, nose and eyes folded into the mud, as well, and there was nothing left of Flint Marko!

Spider-Man crept around the large mud puddle at his feet and looked over to Flash, who lowered the camera and shrugged. The sprinklers kept raining down on them. Officers

Slott and Ramos, peeked through the classroom door and saw their opportunity to get the students out safely. They shuffled them one by one from the classroom to the nearest emergency exit to join the rest of the students and faculty outside where it was safe. Ms. Pranfree, her hair now wet and saggy, took one look at the mud that just moments ago had been a man she'd once known and started to cry. Officer Slott, still injured from the encounter, took her by the arm and led her out the door.

"Is that it? Is it over?" Flash asked. The expanding puddle of mud spread out around Spider-Man's feet. He wanted to tell Flash it was indeed over, but the slight hum of his spider-sense told him otherwise. Then, suddenly, his spider-sense sprang to life — and so did Sandman!

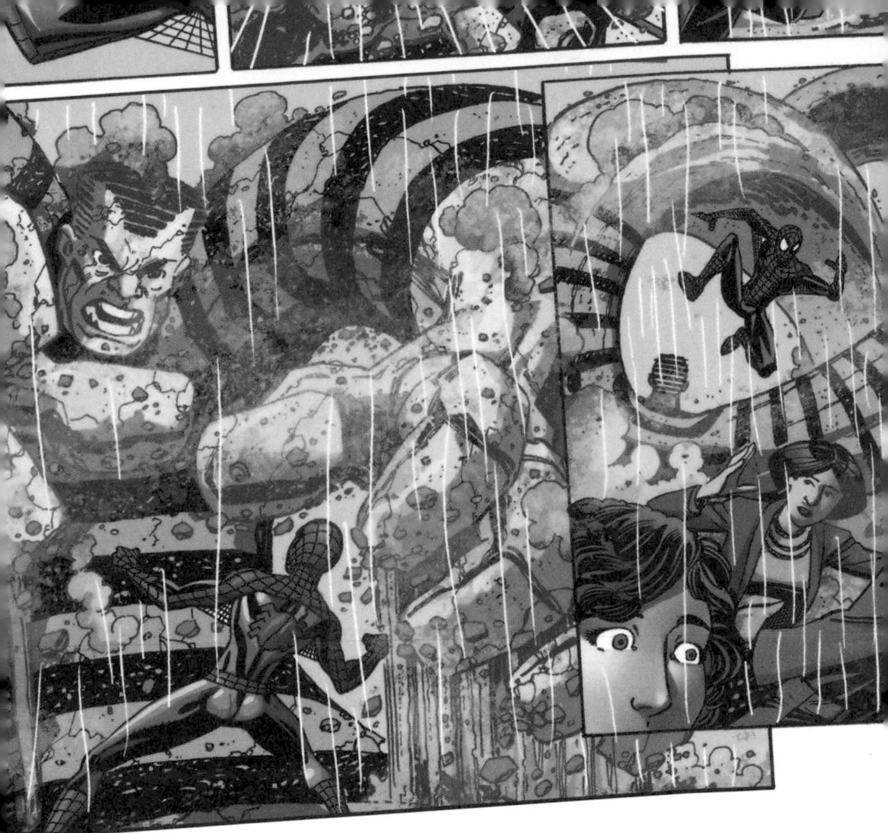

“No, you dummy!” he shouted. “Do I look like the Wicked Witch of the West to you?!” In a split second, Spider-Man was surrounded by a wall of heavy, wet sand. But Sandman’s ruse didn’t work. Spider-Man’s spider-sense gave him just enough time to leap up, cling to the ceiling and jump over Sandman unharmed. Finally in the clear, Spider-Man turned and threw as hard a punch as he could — but his fist went right through Sandman's body! He punched again and again. But Sandman made his body hollow, and Spider-Man's fists flailed hopelessly and harmlessly through him. As long as he was ready for the hit, there was no way Spidey could hurt him. "You're right, " Spider-Man said, "it *is* frustrating when you can't land a punch!"

Sandman laughed and threw a heavy concrete karate chop that would have flattened Spidey like a pancake had he not dodged it at the last

second. But Sandman's laughter was short-lived. His frustration turned to fury.

"You think just because I can't hit you, I can't hurt you?" Sandman said. "Just watch this!" Sandman filled his hand with sand until it was the size of a Buick. But instead of throwing it in Spider-Man's direction, he reached his big mitt across the hall and crushed Flash Thompson into the metal lockers! Again, Uncle Ben's camera fell to the floor.

"NO! FLASH!" Spider-Man yelled. It was his greatest fear come true: A villain he had failed to stop was hurting someone else in his life — just like what happened with Uncle Ben.

And in the brief moment Spider-Man let his guard down, Sandman landed a punch that rocked him across the jaw with the power of a forty-ton

truck. He fell to the floor in a heap,
motionless.

Sandman patted Flash on the
back. Now at his normal size, the
villain walked toward Ms. Pranfree's
classroom. "Thanks for the distraction,
kid," he said. Flash, still struggling for
breath, staggered over to his fallen
hero, who was lying flat on his back.

"Spider-Man?" he said quietly.
"Spidey?" But the wall-crawler, who just
a minute ago wouldn't stand still for
a second, didn't move a muscle. Flash
got down to his knees and tried poking

him in the shoulder, but still nothing. He lowered his ear to Spider-Man's face and listened. He was relieved to hear Spider-Man was still breathing, but he was out cold — which gave Flash an idea.

Ever since he had first heard of Spider-Man, Flash had been curious. All his life, his heroes had been athletes whose accomplishments had been limited to the field. But Spider-Man could do anything the best football and baseball players could do — and much more. He always appeared larger than life in pictures and on television. But seeing him in person, Flash was even more impressed. Spider-Man wasn't big at all. He wasn't even average-sized. He was actually kind of small. Much smaller than Flash expected. Much smaller than Flash himself! He could have been any student at Midtown

High. Whoever he was, Flash figured he must be the best athlete at his school, so surely he would have heard of him. He had to know. After looking around to make sure nobody was watching, he waved his fingers over Spider-Man's face and reached down to peel his mask up from his chin. But before he could touch it, a red-gloved hand reached up and snatched him by the wrist.

"Try it," Spider-Man said, "and I'll make your dentist a rich man."

Flash just smiled. "Spidey! You're all right!"

"I am. Where did he go?"

When Sandman entered the empty classroom, all that was left were some overturned desks, scattered papers and pens, and the StarkTech generator humming as its contacts sparked and crackled on the wet floor.

Sandman looked out the window and saw Ms. Pranfree and her students gathered safely behind a line of police cars. "Oh, Eliza," he said to himself. "You're making this much harder than it has to be." With his attention fixed outside, he never heard Spider-Man coming.

Spider-Man jumped through the doorway and kicked Sandman in the back of the head. "What's the matter, Sandy? Your girlfriend walk out on you?" he said. "I'm surprised, seeing what a cheerful guy you are!" Sandman would have been knocked out cold by Spider-Man's blow had he been an ordinary man, but Flint Marko was far from ordinary. Spider-Man's hardest hit had stunned him a bit, but he was still on his feet!

Spider-Man wasn't sure what to do next. Without the element of surprise, he couldn't lay a hand on him. His best shot wasn't good enough to knock Sandman out, and he was out of options...until he noticed the fully charged contacts of the StarkTech machinery sparking and flopping around on the floor like fish on land. When Sandman

lunged at him, Spidey grabbed the
contacts from the floor and plunged
them deep into his midsection!

Energy is neither created nor
destroyed, Ms. Pranfree had said.
It only changes from one form to
another. When the electrical charge
hit the wet sand, the millions of grains
vibrated. Sandman flared up in white
light so hot it burned Peter's eyes
through his Spider-Man mask. The

force of the heat knocked him down to the floor.

And then, silence. Until...

"Whoa! What did you do?" Flash Thompson said when he entered the room.

Spider-Man lifted his head off the floor to see what had become of Flint Marko, and there he was — standing up with his arms extended and his mouth frozen in a silent scream. Motionless from head to toe, the Sandman had turned into stone.

"I...I think I turned him into a fulgarite," Spider-Man said.

"A what-a-rite?"

"It's a rock formation. It's what you get when lightning strikes sand in the desert or at the beach. I only wanted to stun him, but I guess the sprinkler water mixed into his sand was a strong electrical conductor."

"I'd hate to be Captain Stacy," Flash said, "He's going to have a tough time deciding whether to throw him in jail or put him on display at the art museum."

Officers Slott and Ramos returned with some of their fellow police officers to assess the damage and take statements from the witnesses. Ms. Pranfree told them the story of her ex-boyfriend Flint Marko, who had a good heart but made a lot of bad choices. Marko had been working at her father's store when they fell in love. He had wanted her to have a beautiful engagement ring, but he didn't make enough money to buy one. So one night after the store closed, he had borrowed money from Mr. Pranfree's safe without asking him, hoping to strike it rich at the racetrack. He had been planning to pay it all back after he won. Sadly, Marko had lost every penny. When she had found out, Eliza Pranfree had broken up with him, but he had vowed to win her back by replacing the money. After every effort had failed, he had resorted to robbing a bank. A few hours later, the police had caught

up to him and cornered him on the beach. That's when he had been turned into Sandman.

Across the room, Spider-Man was still examining the fulgarite of Sandman. Was Flint Marko alive in there? Could he hear what they were saying? If he was able to exist as a living pile of sand, why not as a fulgarite? After all, energy can't be created or destroyed — it just changes form, right?

"Hey, Spidey, aren't you forgetting something?"

Flash Thompson tossed Spider-Man the camera. "I don't think you want to leave this behind. It seems pretty important to you.

"What did you need the pictures for anyway?"

"Uh...scrapbooking! It's sort of my passion," Spider-Man replied.

"I wouldn't have told anyone, you know," Flash said.

"Huh?"

"Who you really are under the mask. I would have kept it a secret."

"I know," Spider-Man said.

"'Scuse me, Spider-Man," Officer Slott interrupted. "Sorry about this, but...I'm afraid I have to take you in."

"WHAT?!" Spidey and Flash said at the same time.

"Because of all the negative press from *The Daily Bugle*, the mayor's putting pressure on us to lock you up — seein' that you're a masked vigilante and all."

Spider-Man and Flash looked at each other in disbelief. After all the good Spider-Man had done, he was about to be arrested by the police! So he did the only thing he could. He jumped out the window while Flash blocked Officer Slott like it was football practice. "Run, Spidey, run!" Flash shouted. And he did, all the way to Aunt May's house without looking back.

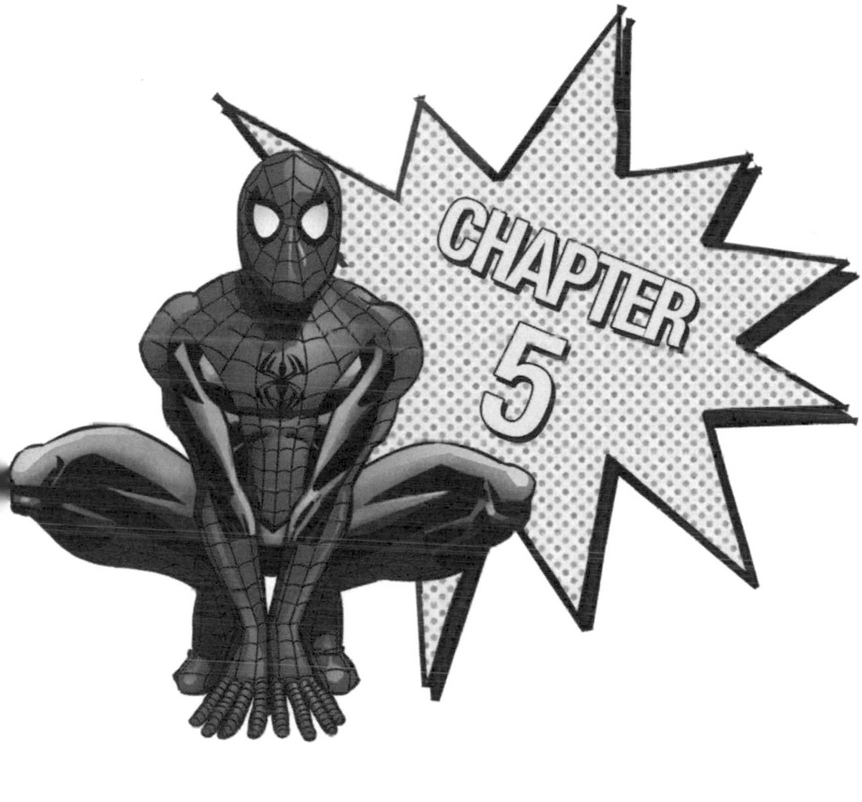
CHAPTER
5

Mr. Rodriguez looked disappointed. He turned to face the wall and released the ball from his fingers. It bounced off the wall with a loud KA-THUNK! and returned to him. "I thought you said you were going to tell me the truth," he said.

"What do you mean? I just told you what happened."

"Peter," Mr. Rodriguez turned to face him again. "Flash isn't the only one who said you ran out of the room. Several other students said the same thing. So how would you know about anything that happened when the only people there were Sandman, Flash and Spider-Man?"

Peter got quiet. How could he be so foolish? Unless he revealed to Mr. Rodriguez he was really Spider-Man, there was no way to explain how he knew what happened and prove he wasn't the coward Flash made him out to be.

"For the past few weeks you've been showing up late for school. And when you *are* here, you sleep through class. You ran out of the room before anyone else, right before Spider-Man showed up. And you never did explain to me how you got that black eye," Mr. Rodriguez said. "I think I know what's going on here."

Peter swallowed hard. His heart pounded. Could it be? Did Mr. Rodriguez know his secret?

"I think you have PTSD."

"What?" Peter said.

"Post-Traumatic Stress Disorder. You know, from your Uncle Ben's passing. It all adds up. Your bad school habits started right after his funeral. You probably had a panic attack in class when the police showed up, and that's why you rushed past your classmates to get away. You won't tell me what happened to your eye because you're probably ashamed to tell me you did it to yourself.

"Your symptoms are very common to PTSD. Most people don't realize it's very common in children who experience a traumatic event.

"Why don't we meet again next week? I can recommend some people you can talk to who may be able to help. If you want, I can call in your Aunt May, and the three of us can..."

Peter had heard enough. He sprang from the chair, threw his backpack over his shoulder and was on his way out the door.

"Peter, what are you doing?"

"I'm leaving," he said. "You called me in to talk about the Sandman, not about...this."

"No," Mr. Rodriguez said. "*You* came in to talk about the Sandman. *I* wanted to talk to you about falling asleep in class."

But Peter wouldn't hear it. "And I really don't think my Aunt May would appreciate the football coach butting in on our personal matters," he said, ready to escape to the hallways.

"Who do you think asked me to talk to you about it?" Mr. Rodriguez called out.

Peter stopped. *Aunt May? Is it possible?* he thought. *There's no way.*

"She's worried about you, Peter. I know you're upset about losing your Uncle Ben, but you can't forget she lost her husband. You're all she's got.

She said you haven't been home much. You've been keeping secrets.

"What you've been through is a lot for a 16-year-old to bear. You don't have to do it alone. You can't do it alone."

Peter was angry. It wasn't that he thought Mr. Rodriguez was wrong. It was that he knew he was right. The nightmares were constant. And he did push his classmates out of the way while Flash Thompson helped them evacuate. He was so desperate for Spider-Man to stop the Sandman the way he didn't stop Uncle Ben's killer, he forgot his responsibility should have been to protect his classmates.

When Uncle Ben was still alive, Peter could talk to him about

anything. Now, with his uncle gone, he felt alone. But Mr. Rodriguez was right. He didn't have to be.

"Don't worry about Flash and the other guys," Mr. Rodriguez said. "They'll lay off you, I promise. Just go home and talk to your aunt. Tell her what's going on."

It was a long walk home. Normally after school, he'd go on patrol as

Spider-Man for a while. But Peter decided to do some thinking, instead.

"Peter, dear, is that you?" asked Aunt May when he walked into the apartment. "You don't usually come right home. Is everything all right?"

"I talked to Mr. Rodriguez today, Aunt May."

Aunt May pouted. "I'm so sorry, I know you don't like when I pry...it's just you seem so lost. I didn't know what else to do."

"It's all right, Aunt May. He's right. *You're* right. I've been so wrapped up in my own stuff, I forgot you've been through a lot, too. We can't go it alone. With Uncle Ben gone, we have to be there for each other. I'm sorry I let you down." Peter wrapped his arms around Aunt May and squeezed her close.

"You know better than that, Peter," Aunt May said and kissed him on the forehead. "You could never let me down. Ever.

"That Mr. Rodriguez is a very nice man, isn't he?"

"He is," Peter said. "And I'll tell him you said so when I meet with him again next week."

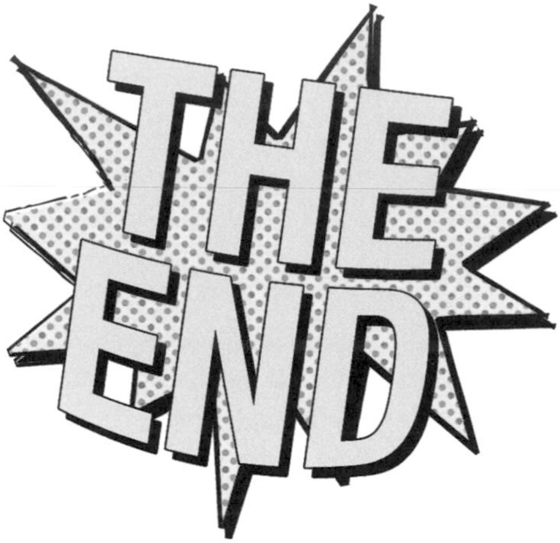
THE END

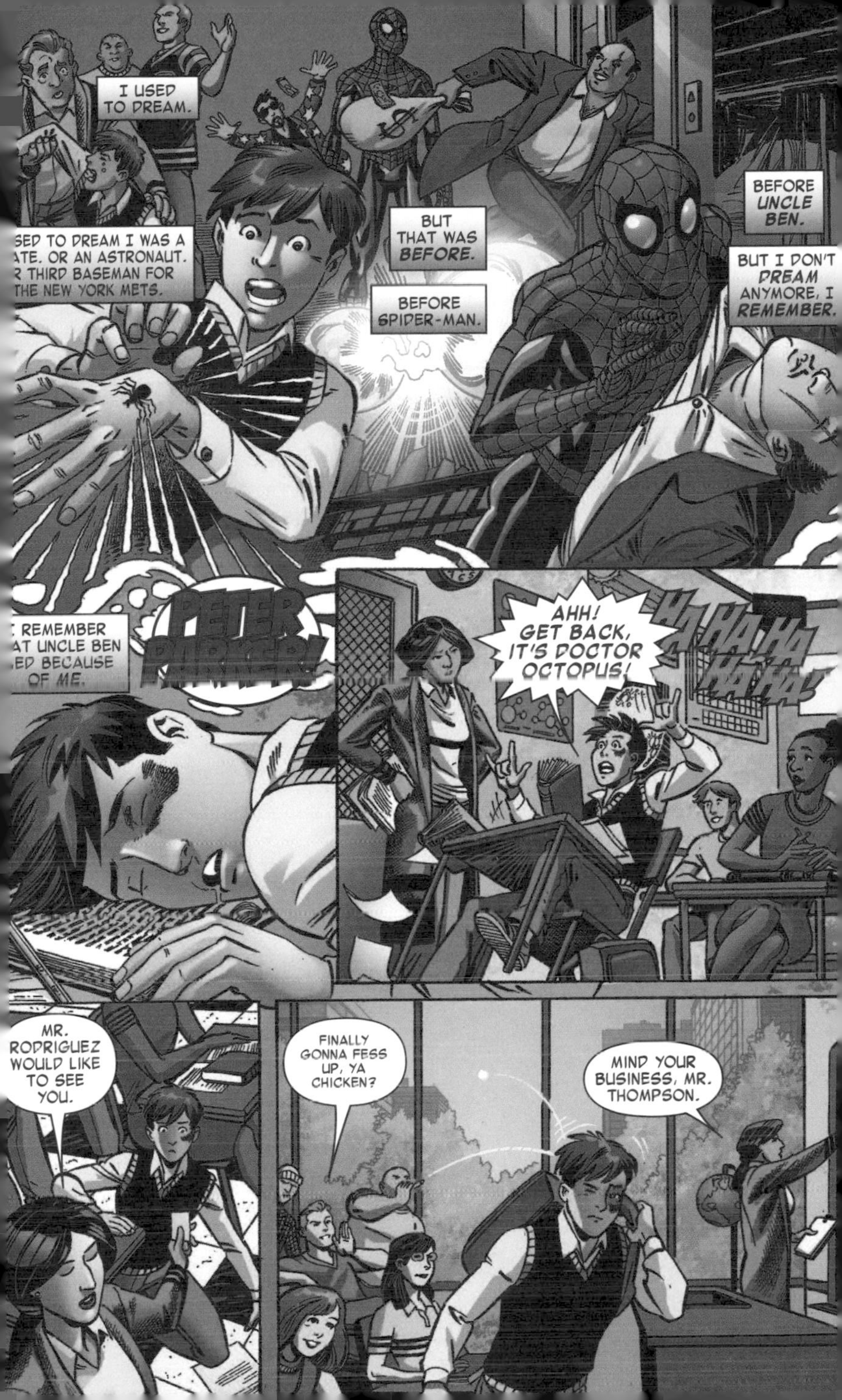
I USED TO DREAM.
SED TO DREAM I WAS A
ATE. OR AN ASTRONAUT.
R THIRD BASEMAN FOR
THE NEW YORK METS.
BUT THAT WAS BEFORE.
BEFORE SPIDER-MAN.
BEFORE UNCLE BEN.
BUT I DON'T DREAM ANYMORE, I REMEMBER.
REMEMBER
AT UNCLE BEN
ED BECAUSE
OF ME.
PETER
AHH! GET BACK, IT'S DOCTOR OCTOPUS!
HA HA HA HA HA!
MR. RODRIGUEZ WOULD LIKE TO SEE YOU.
FINALLY GONNA FESS UP, YA CHICKEN?
MIND YOUR BUSINESS, MR. THOMPSON.

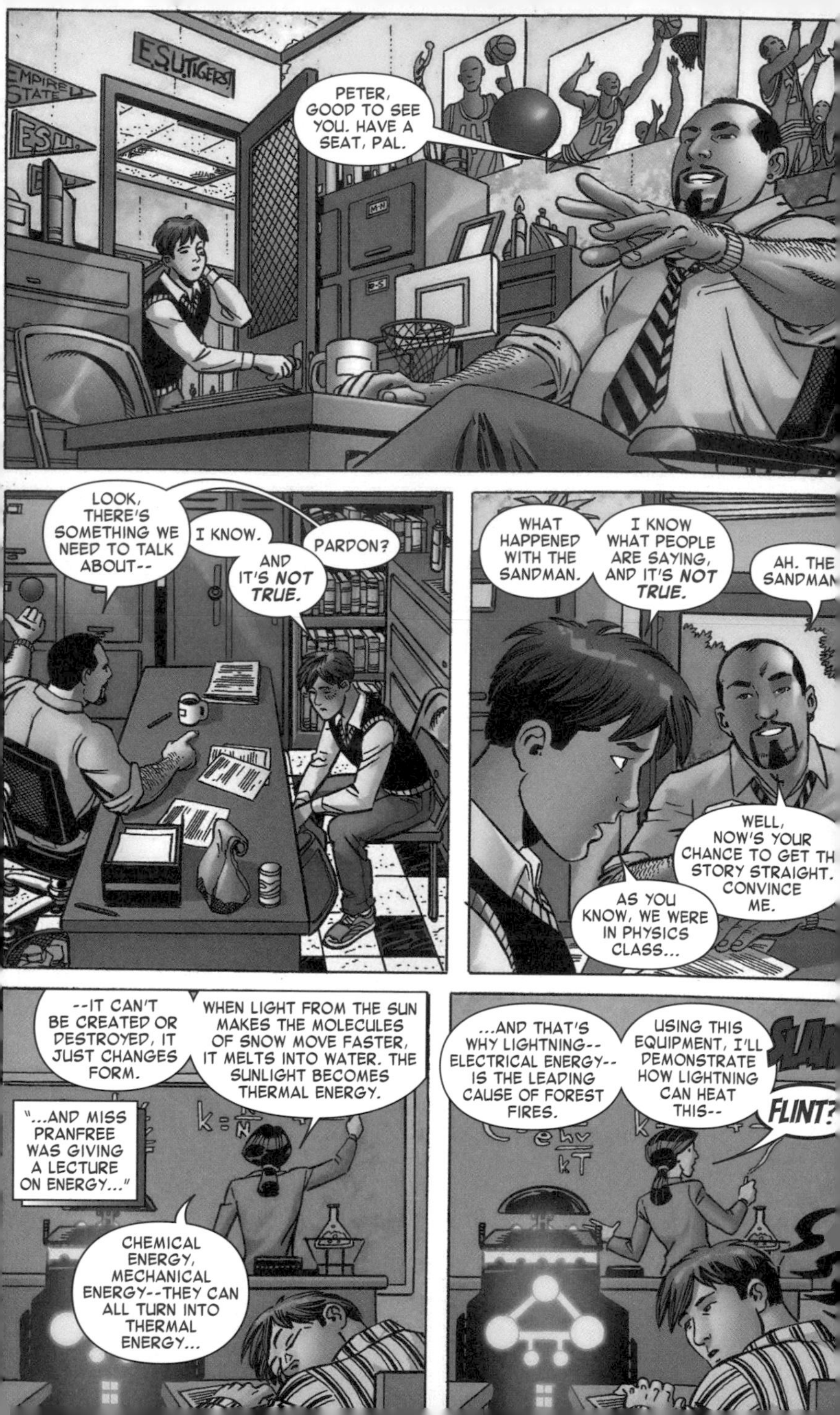
E.S.U. TIGERS!
EMPIRE STATE
ESU
PETER, GOOD TO SEE YOU. HAVE A SEAT, PAL.
LOOK, THERE'S SOMETHING WE NEED TO TALK ABOUT--
I KNOW.
PARDON?
AND IT'S *NOT TRUE.*
WHAT HAPPENED WITH THE SANDMAN.
I KNOW WHAT PEOPLE ARE SAYING, AND IT'S *NOT TRUE.*
AH. THE SANDMAN
WELL, NOW'S YOUR CHANCE TO GET TH STORY STRAIGHT. CONVINCE ME.
AS YOU KNOW, WE WERE IN PHYSICS CLASS...
"...AND MISS PRANFREE WAS GIVING A LECTURE ON ENERGY..."
--IT CAN'T BE CREATED OR DESTROYED, IT JUST CHANGES FORM.
WHEN LIGHT FROM THE SUN MAKES THE MOLECULES OF SNOW MOVE FASTER, IT MELTS INTO WATER. THE SUNLIGHT BECOMES THERMAL ENERGY.
CHEMICAL ENERGY, MECHANICAL ENERGY--THEY CAN ALL TURN INTO THERMAL ENERGY...
...AND THAT'S WHY LIGHTNING--ELECTRICAL ENERGY--IS THE LEADING CAUSE OF FOREST FIRES.
USING THIS EQUIPMENT, I'LL DEMONSTRATE HOW LIGHTNING CAN HEAT THIS--
SLAM
FLINT?

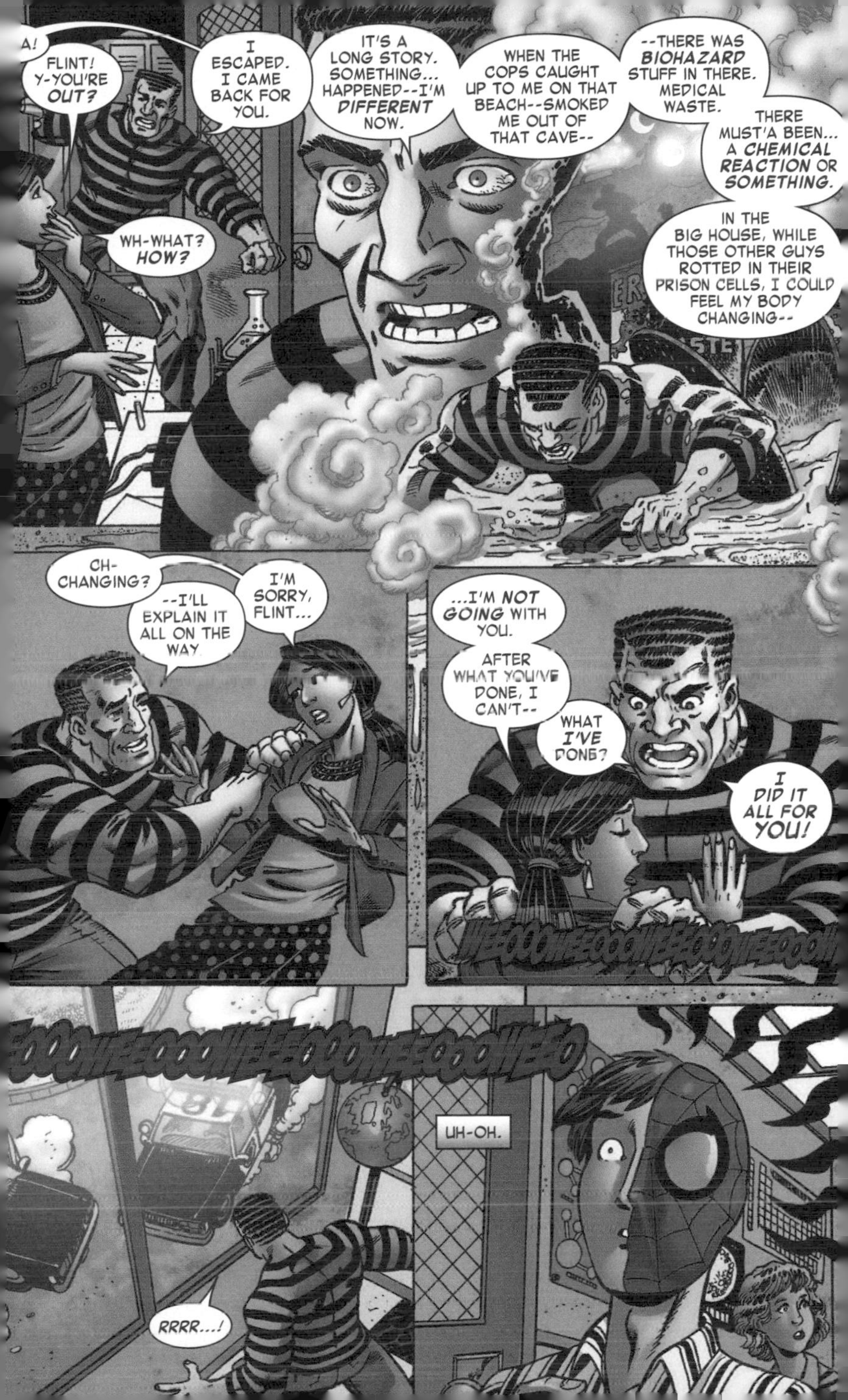
A!
FLINT! Y-YOU'RE OUT?
I ESCAPED. I CAME BACK FOR YOU.
WH-WHAT? HOW?
IT'S A LONG STORY. SOMETHING... HAPPENED--I'M DIFFERENT NOW.
WHEN THE COPS CAUGHT UP TO ME ON THAT BEACH--SMOKED ME OUT OF THAT CAVE--
--THERE WAS BIOHAZARD STUFF IN THERE. MEDICAL WASTE.
THERE MUST'A BEEN... A CHEMICAL REACTION OR SOMETHING.
IN THE BIG HOUSE, WHILE THOSE OTHER GUYS ROTTED IN THEIR PRISON CELLS, I COULD FEEL MY BODY CHANGING--
CH-CHANGING?
--I'LL EXPLAIN IT ALL ON THE WAY.
I'M SORRY, FLINT...
...I'M NOT GOING WITH YOU.
AFTER WHAT YOU'VE DONE, I CAN'T--
WHAT I'VE DONE?
I DID IT ALL FOR YOU!
WEEOOOWEEOOOWEEOOOWEEOOOW
EOOOWEEOOOWEEOOOWEEOOOWEEO
UH-OH.
RRRR...!

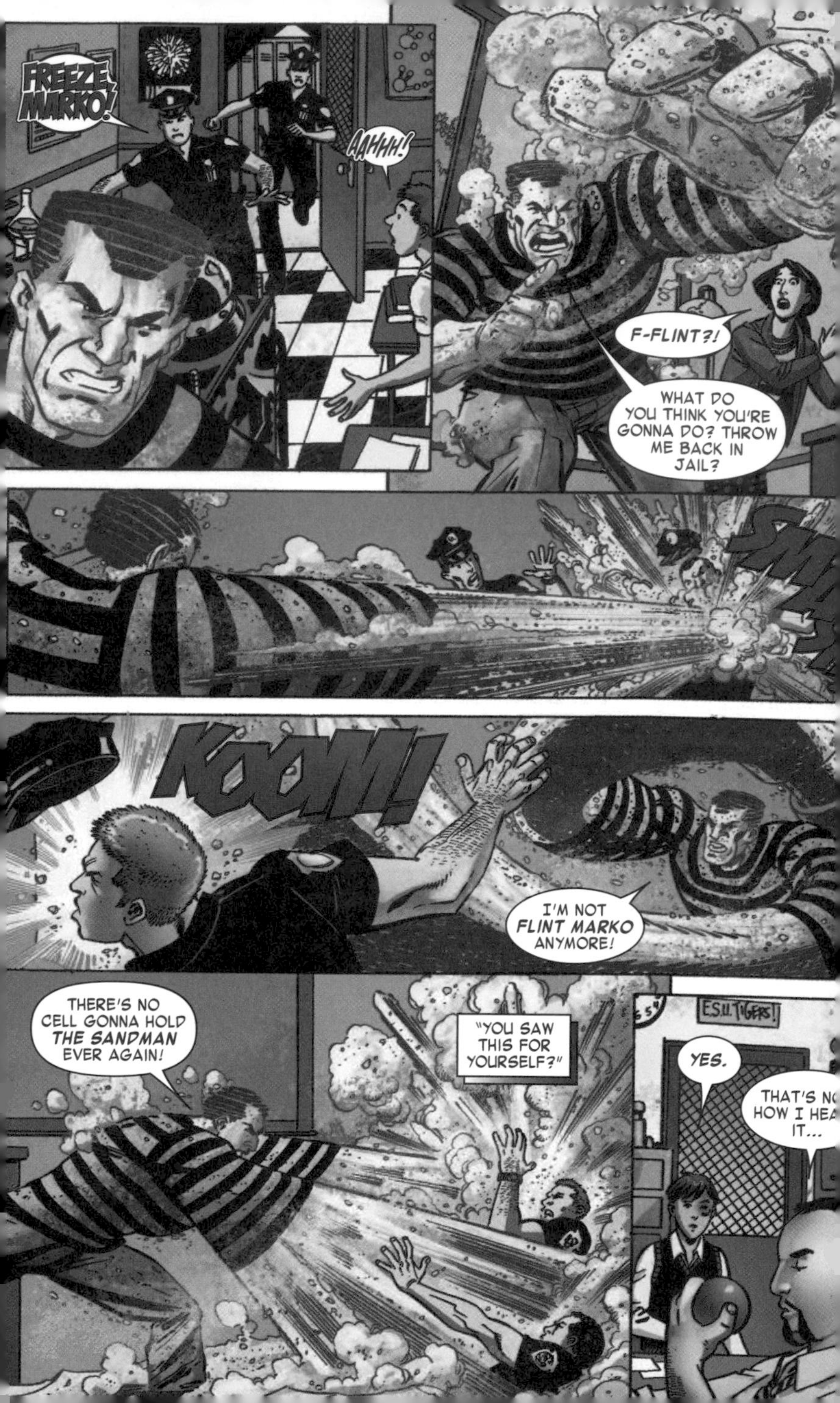
FREEZE, MARKO!
AAHHH!
F-FLINT?!
WHAT DO YOU THINK YOU'RE GONNA DO? THROW ME BACK IN JAIL?
KOOM!
I'M NOT FLINT MARKO ANYMORE!
THERE'S NO CELL GONNA HOLD THE SANDMAN EVER AGAIN!
"YOU SAW THIS FOR YOURSELF?"
E.S.U. TIGERS!
YES.

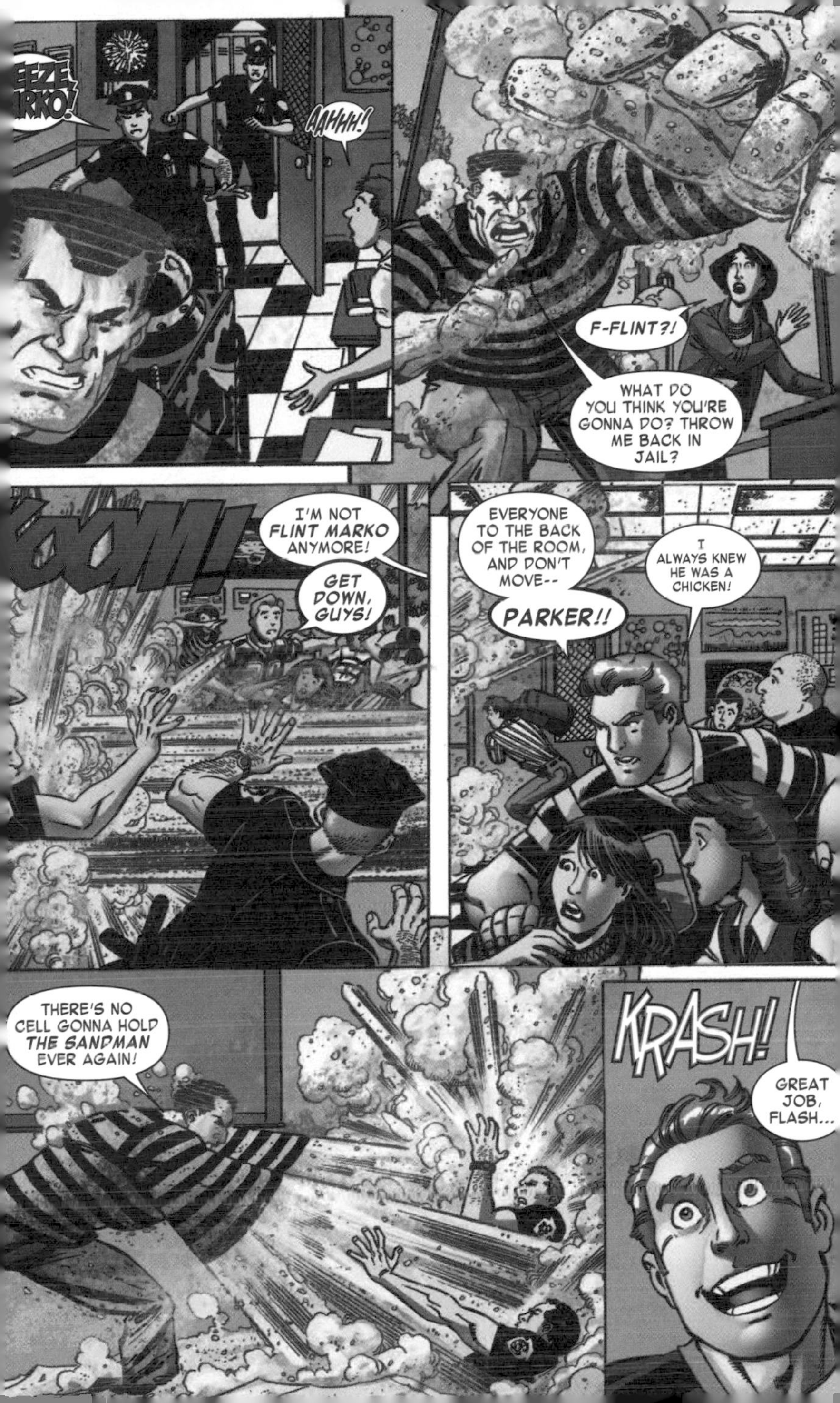

EEZE ARKO!
AAHHH!
F-FLINT?!
WHAT DO YOU THINK YOU'RE GONNA DO? THROW ME BACK IN JAIL?
OOM!
I'M NOT FLINT MARKO ANYMORE!
GET DOWN, GUYS!
EVERYONE TO THE BACK OF THE ROOM, AND DON'T MOVE--
PARKER!!
I ALWAYS KNEW HE WAS A CHICKEN!
THERE'S NO CELL GONNA HOLD THE SANDMAN EVER AGAIN!
KRASH!
GREAT JOB, FLASH...

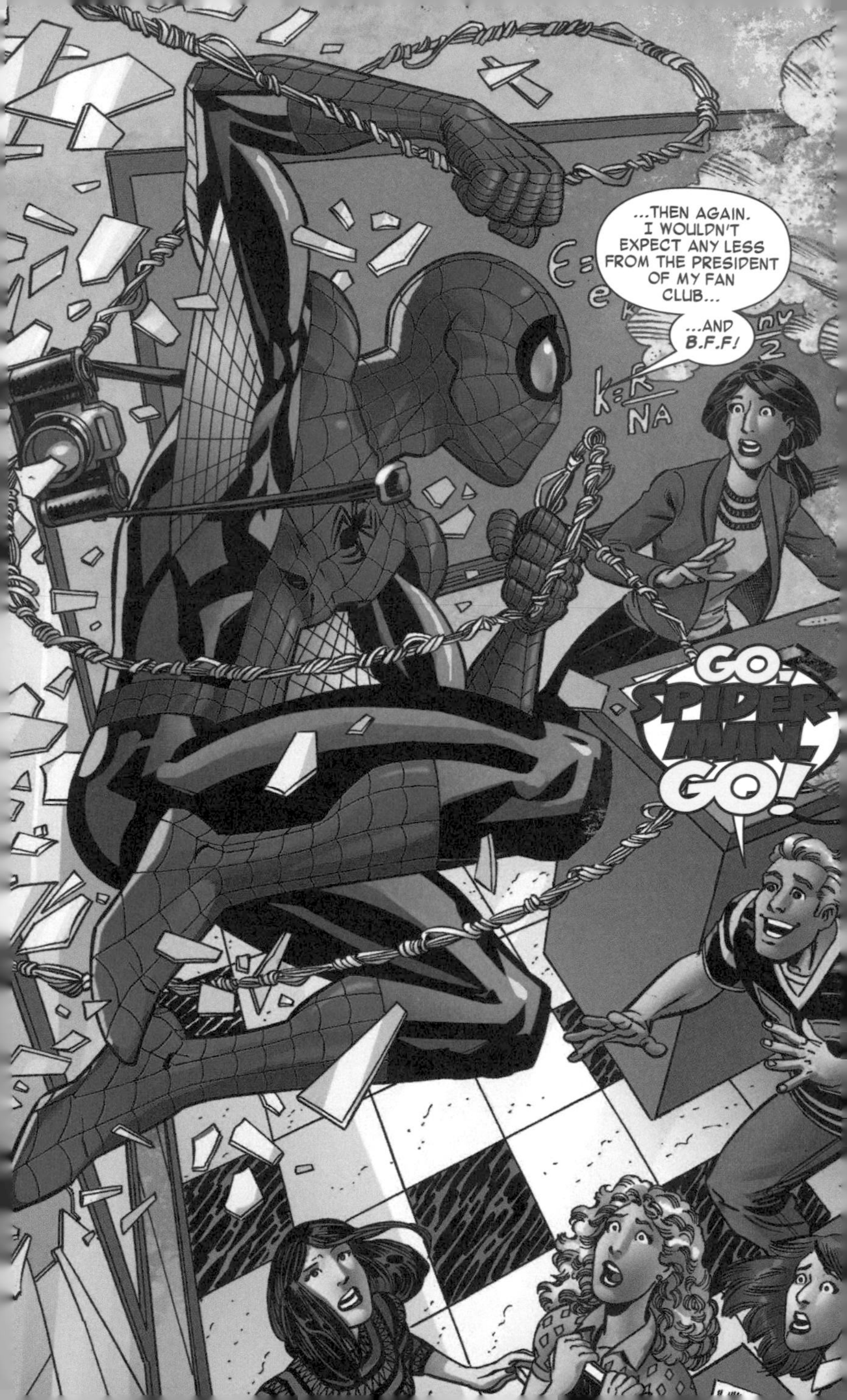
...THEN AGAIN. I WOULDN'T EXPECT ANY LESS FROM THE PRESIDENT OF MY FAN CLUB...
...AND B.F.F!
GO, SPIDER-MAN, GO!

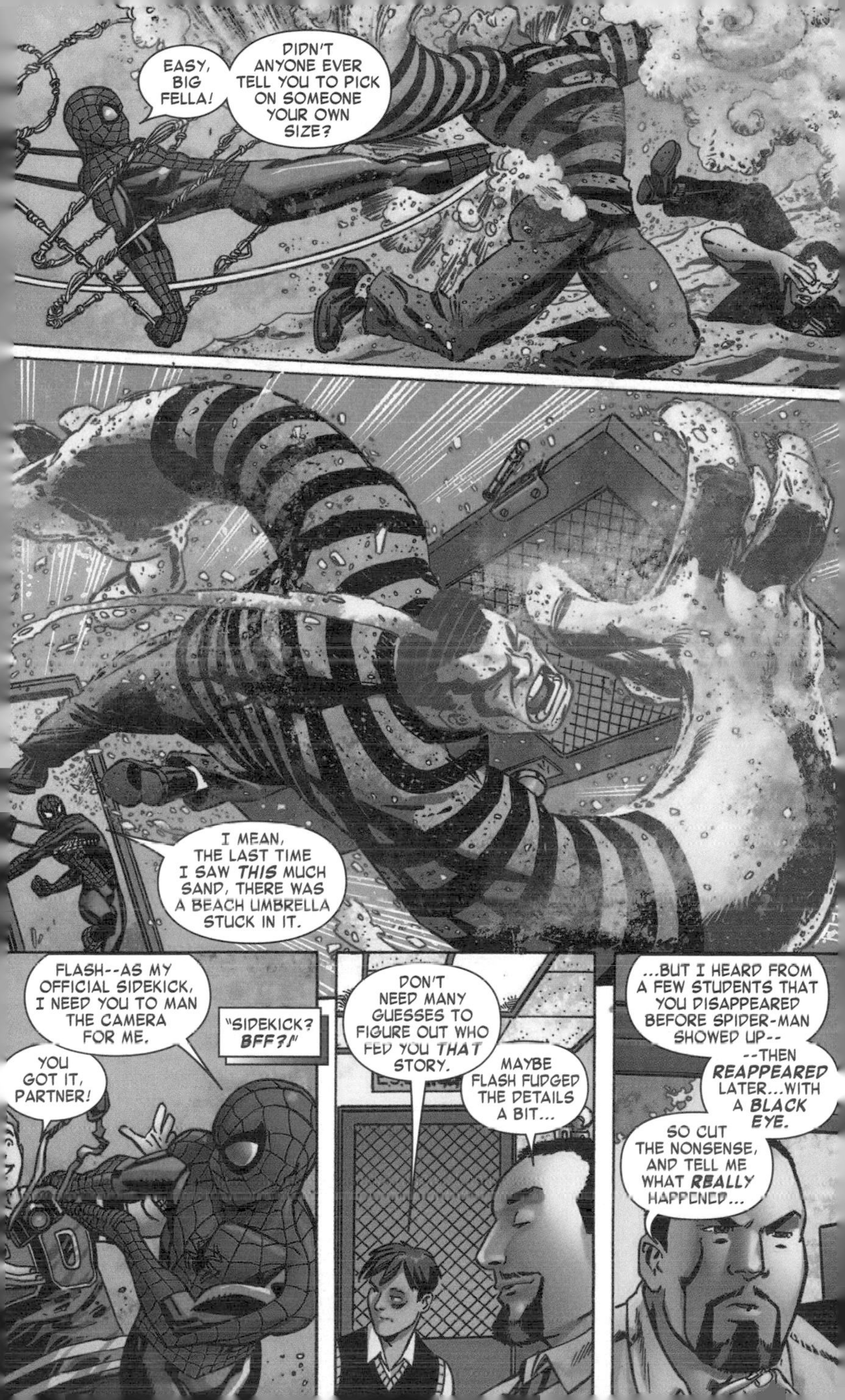
EASY, BIG FELLA!
DIDN'T ANYONE EVER TELL YOU TO PICK ON SOMEONE YOUR OWN SIZE?
I MEAN, THE LAST TIME I SAW THIS MUCH SAND, THERE WAS A BEACH UMBRELLA STUCK IN IT.
FLASH--AS MY OFFICIAL SIDEKICK, I NEED YOU TO MAN THE CAMERA FOR ME.
YOU GOT IT, PARTNER!
"SIDEKICK? BFF?!"
DON'T NEED MANY GUESSES TO FIGURE OUT WHO FED YOU THAT STORY.
MAYBE FLASH FUDGED THE DETAILS A BIT...
...BUT I HEARD FROM A FEW STUDENTS THAT YOU DISAPPEARED BEFORE SPIDER-MAN SHOWED UP--
--THEN REAPPEARED LATER...WITH A BLACK EYE.
SO CUT THE NONSENSE, AND TELL ME WHAT REALLY HAPPENED...

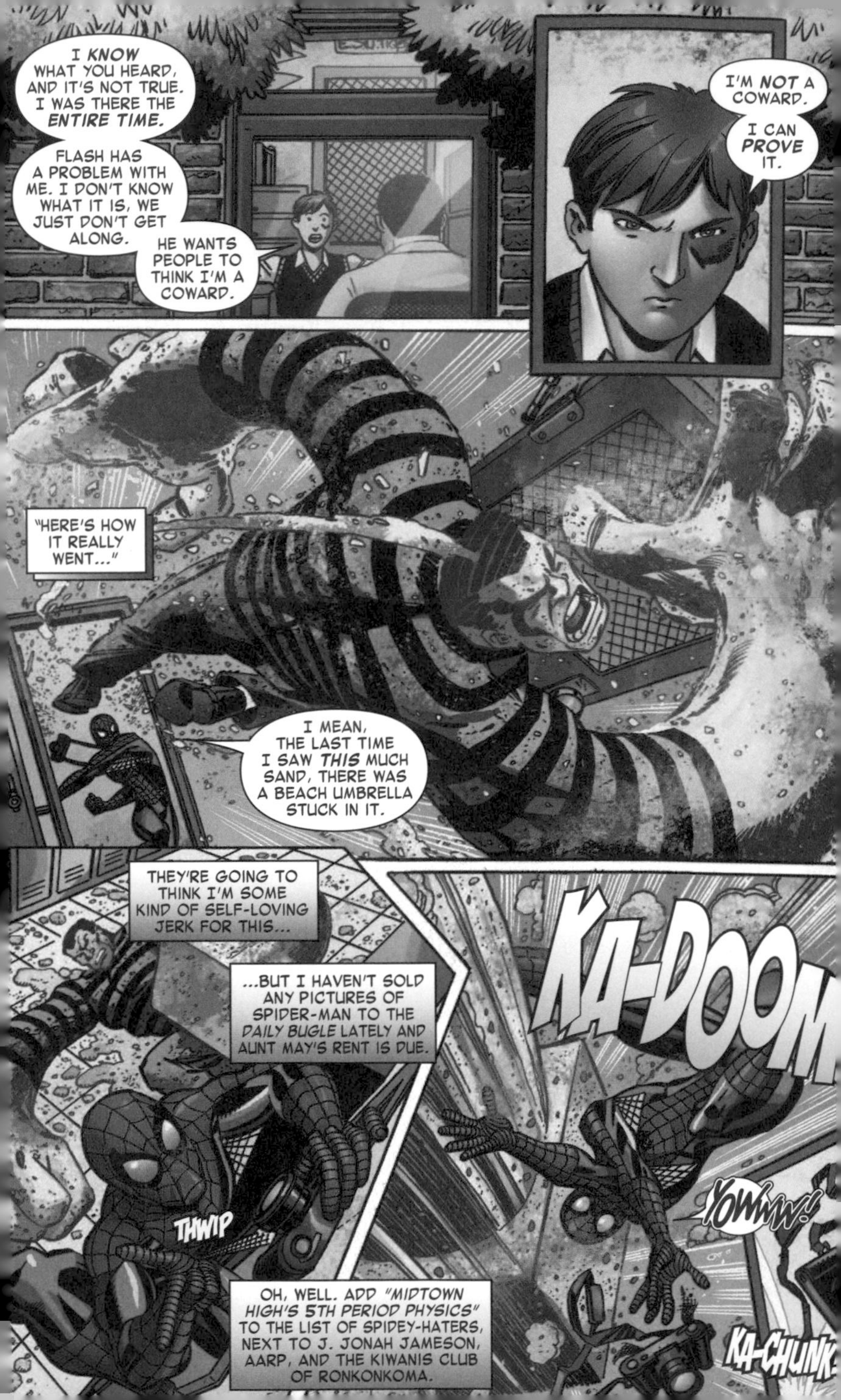
I *KNOW* WHAT YOU HEARD, AND IT'S NOT TRUE. I WAS THERE THE *ENTIRE TIME.*
FLASH HAS A PROBLEM WITH ME. I DON'T KNOW WHAT IT IS, WE JUST DON'T GET ALONG.
HE WANTS PEOPLE TO THINK I'M A COWARD.
I'M *NOT* A COWARD.
I CAN *PROVE* IT.
"HERE'S HOW IT REALLY WENT..."
I MEAN, THE LAST TIME I SAW *THIS* MUCH SAND, THERE WAS A BEACH UMBRELLA STUCK IN IT.
THEY'RE GOING TO THINK I'M SOME KIND OF SELF-LOVING JERK FOR THIS...
...BUT I HAVEN'T SOLD ANY PICTURES OF SPIDER-MAN TO THE *DAILY BUGLE* LATELY AND AUNT MAY'S RENT IS DUE.
KA-DOOM
THWIP
YOWWW!
OH, WELL. ADD *"MIDTOWN HIGH'S 5TH PERIOD PHYSICS"* TO THE LIST OF SPIDEY-HATERS, NEXT TO J. JONAH JAMESON, AARP, AND THE KIWANIS CLUB OF RONKONKOMA.
KA-CHUNK

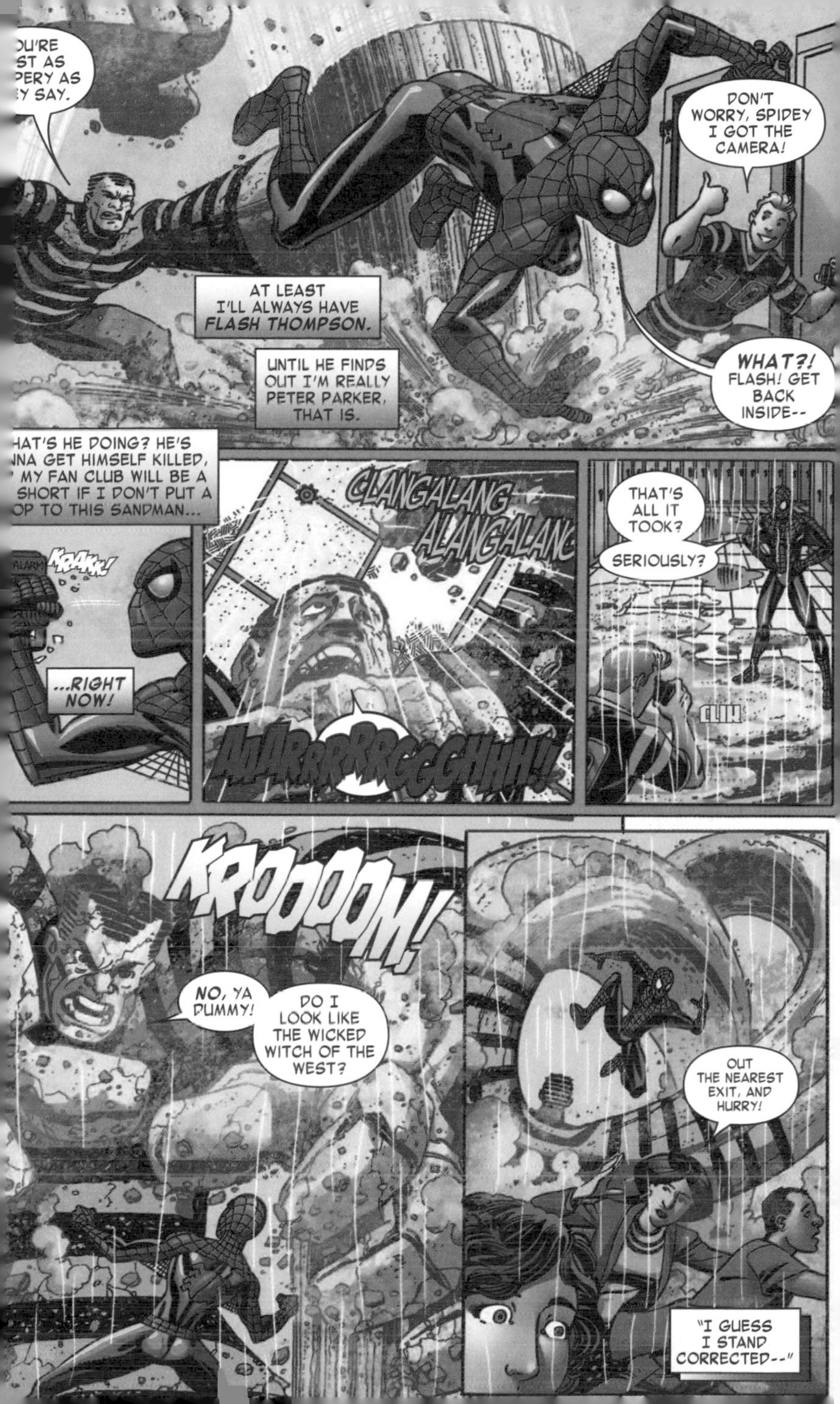

OU'RE
ST AS
PERY AS
Y SAY.
DON'T
WORRY, SPIDEY
I GOT THE
CAMERA!
AT LEAST
I'LL ALWAYS HAVE
FLASH THOMPSON.
UNTIL HE FINDS
OUT I'M REALLY
PETER PARKER,
THAT IS.
WHAT?!
FLASH! GET
BACK
INSIDE--
HAT'S HE DOING? HE'S
NNA GET HIMSELF KILLED,
MY FAN CLUB WILL BE A
SHORT IF I DON'T PUT A
OP TO THIS SANDMAN...
KRAKK!
ALARM
...RIGHT
NOW!
CLANGALANG
ALANGALANG
AAARRRRRGGGHHH!!
THAT'S
ALL IT
TOOK?
SERIOUSLY?
CLIK
KROOOOM!
NO, YA
DUMMY!
DO I
LOOK LIKE
THE WICKED
WITCH OF THE
WEST?
OUT
THE NEAREST
EXIT, AND
HURRY!
"I GUESS
I STAND
CORRECTED--"

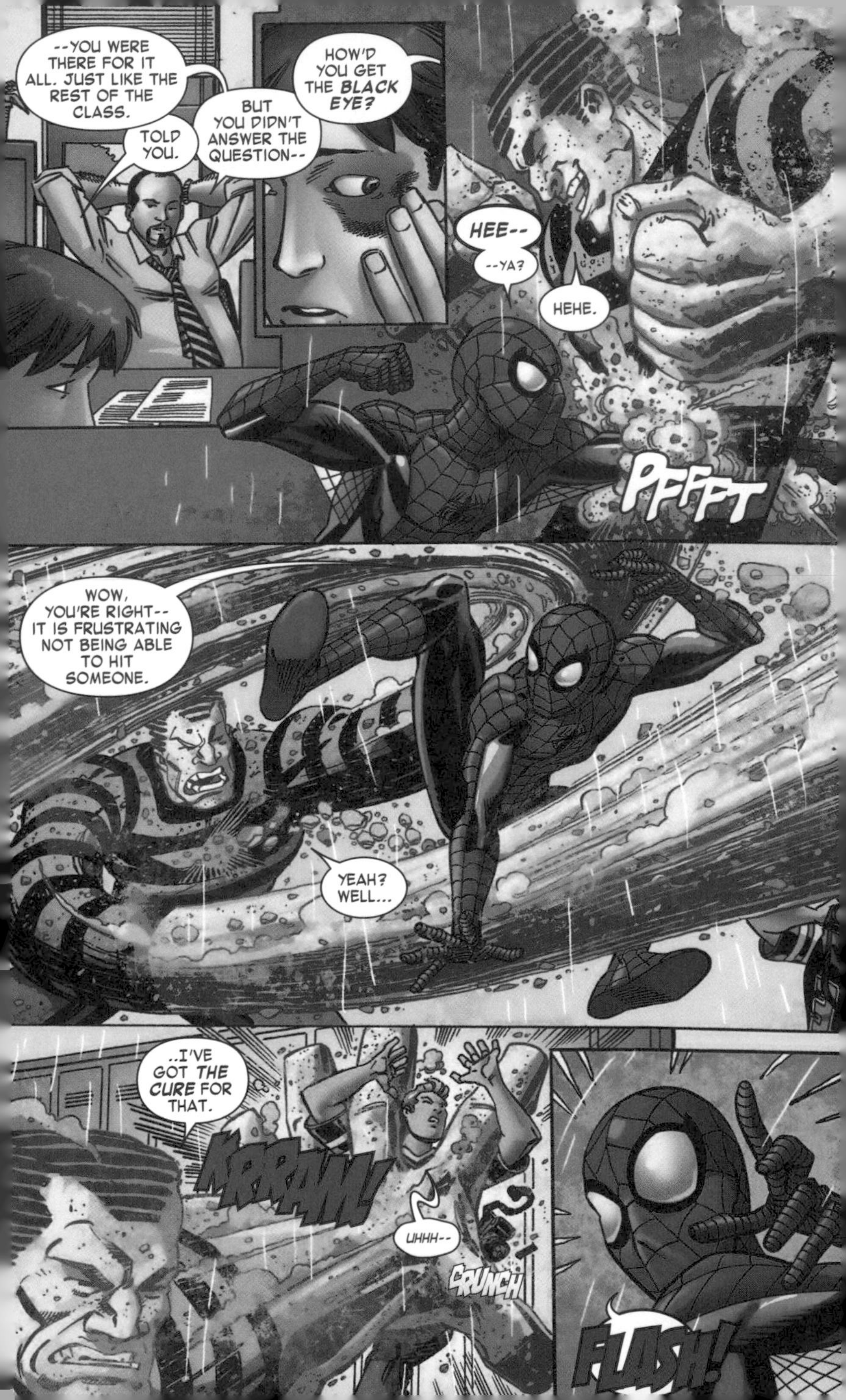

--YOU WERE THERE FOR IT ALL. JUST LIKE THE REST OF THE CLASS.
TOLD YOU.
BUT YOU DIDN'T ANSWER THE QUESTION--
HOW'D YOU GET THE BLACK EYE?
HEE--
--YA?
HEHE.
PFFFT
WOW, YOU'RE RIGHT-- IT IS FRUSTRATING NOT BEING ABLE TO HIT SOMEONE.
YEAH? WELL...
..I'VE GOT THE CURE FOR THAT.
KRRAM!
UHHH--
CRUNCH
FLASH!

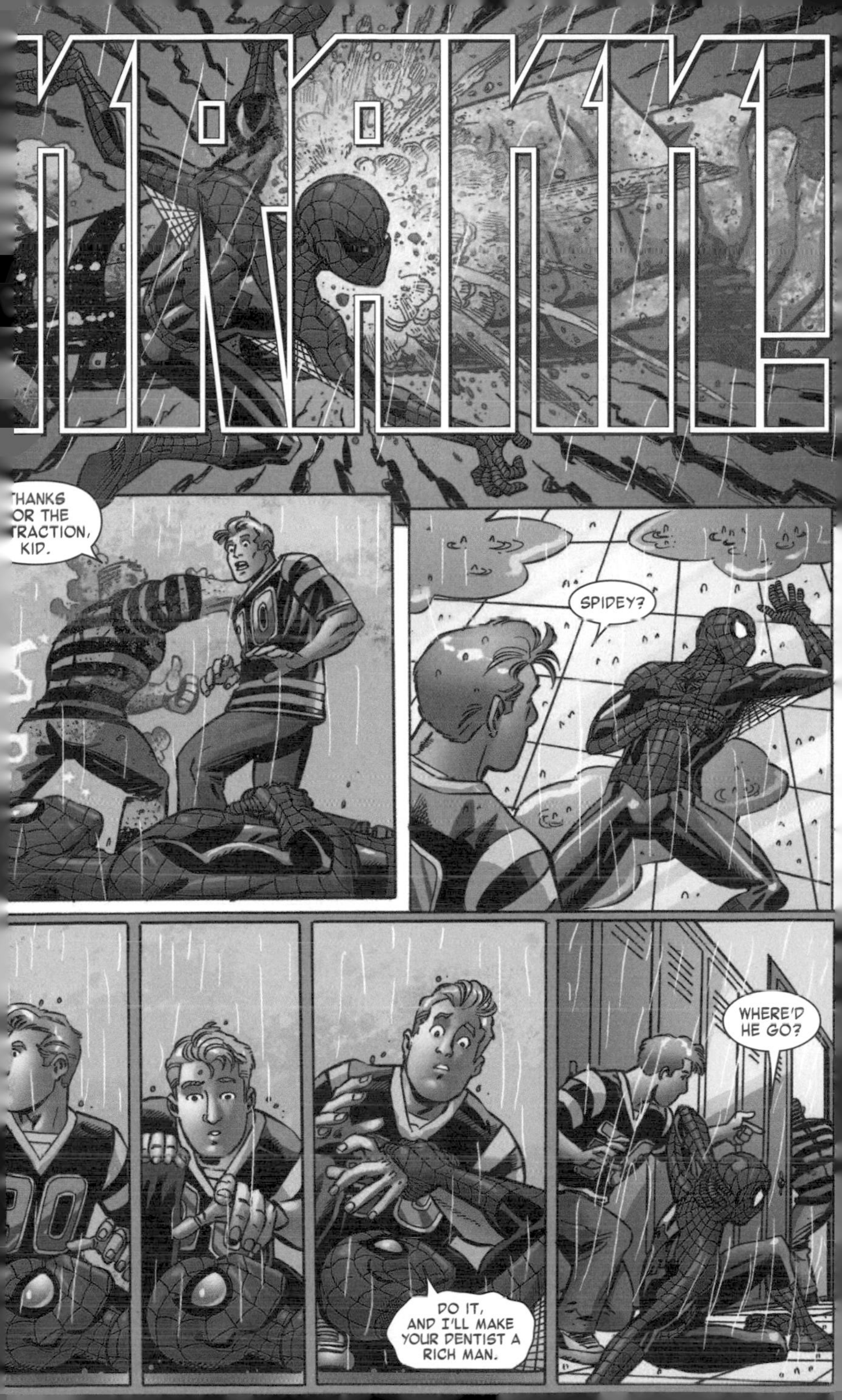
KRAKK!
THANKS
OR THE
TRACTION,
KID.
SPIDEY?
DO IT, AND I'LL MAKE YOUR DENTIST A RICH MAN.
WHERE'D HE GO?

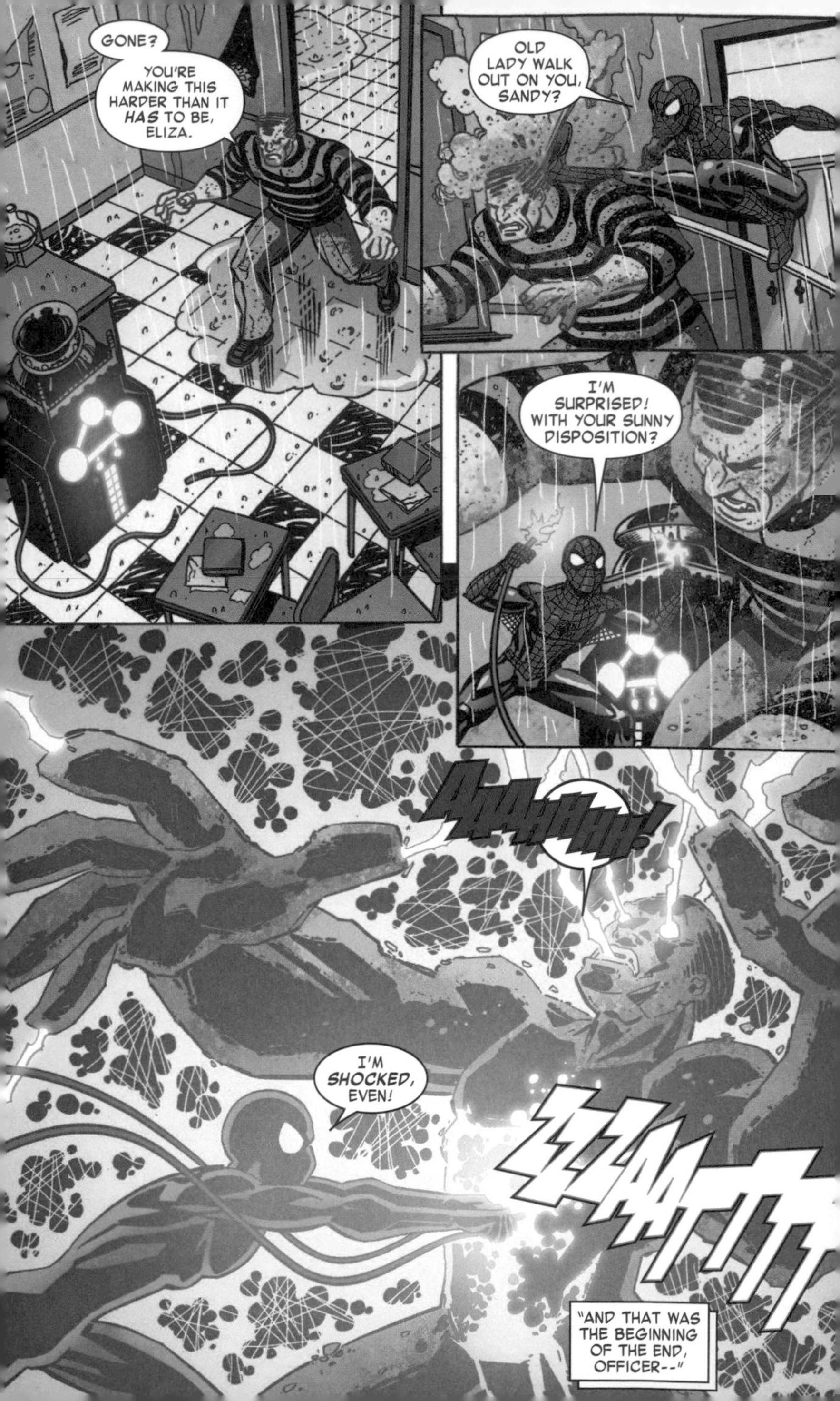
GONE?
YOU'RE MAKING THIS HARDER THAN IT HAS TO BE, ELIZA.
OLD LADY WALK OUT ON YOU, SANDY?
I'M SURPRISED! WITH YOUR SUNNY DISPOSITION?
AAAHHHH!
I'M SHOCKED, EVEN!
ZZZAAATTT
"AND THAT WAS THE BEGINNING OF THE END, OFFICER--"

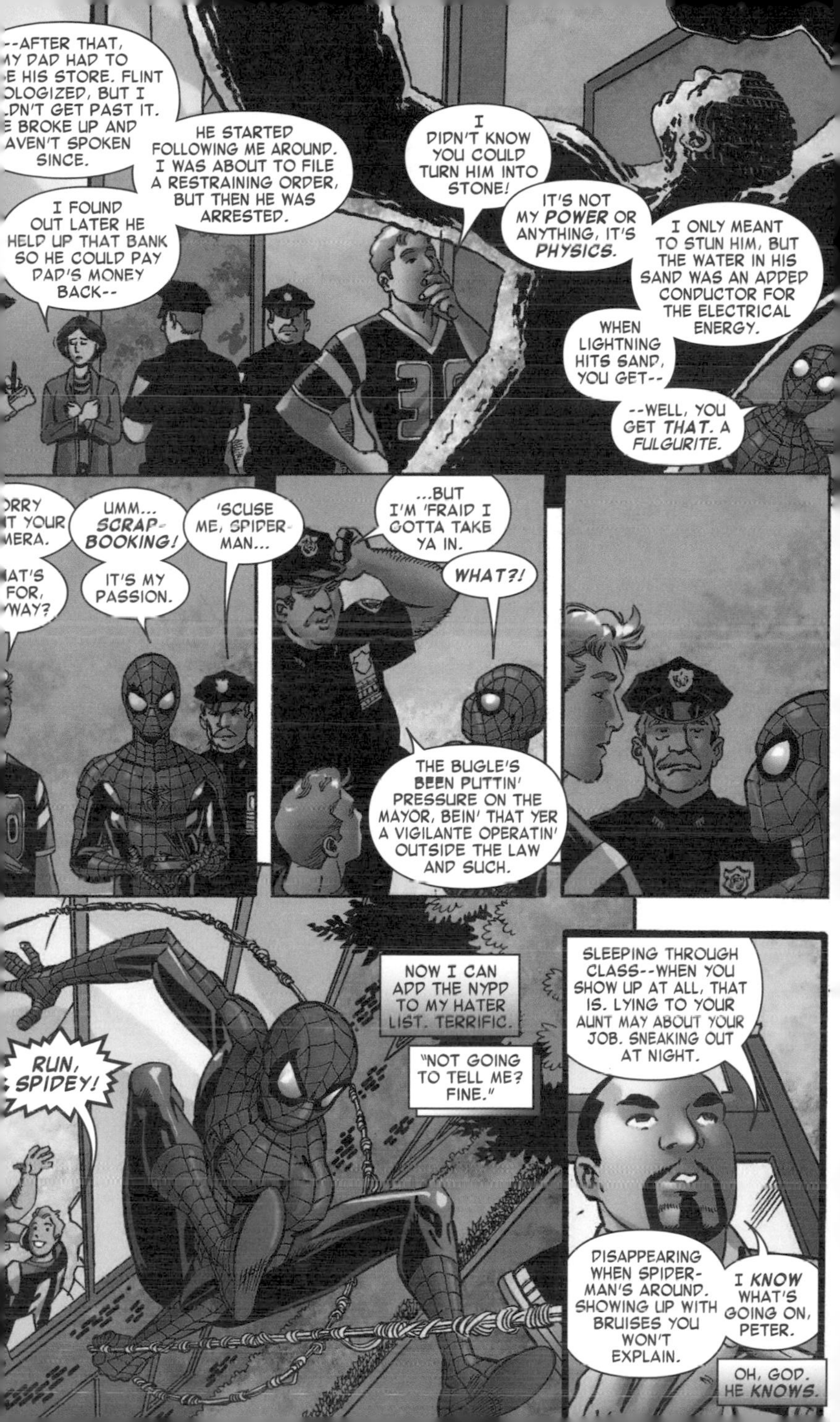
--AFTER THAT, MY DAD HAD TO E HIS STORE. FLINT OLOGIZED, BUT I DN'T GET PAST IT. E BROKE UP AND AVEN'T SPOKEN SINCE.
HE STARTED FOLLOWING ME AROUND. I WAS ABOUT TO FILE A RESTRAINING ORDER, BUT THEN HE WAS ARRESTED.
I FOUND OUT LATER HE HELD UP THAT BANK SO HE COULD PAY DAD'S MONEY BACK--
I DIDN'T KNOW YOU COULD TURN HIM INTO STONE!
IT'S NOT MY POWER OR ANYTHING, IT'S PHYSICS.
I ONLY MEANT TO STUN HIM, BUT THE WATER IN HIS SAND WAS AN ADDED CONDUCTOR FOR THE ELECTRICAL ENERGY.
WHEN LIGHTNING HITS SAND, YOU GET--
--WELL, YOU GET THAT. A FULGURITE.
ORRY IT YOUR MERA.
IAT'S FOR, WAY?
UMM... SCRAP-BOOKING!
IT'S MY PASSION.
'SCUSE ME, SPIDER-MAN...
...BUT I'M 'FRAID I GOTTA TAKE YA IN.
WHAT?!
THE BUGLE'S BEEN PUTTIN' PRESSURE ON THE MAYOR, BEIN' THAT YER A VIGILANTE OPERATIN' OUTSIDE THE LAW AND SUCH.
RUN, SPIDEY!
NOW I CAN ADD THE NYPD TO MY HATER LIST. TERRIFIC.
"NOT GOING TO TELL ME? FINE."
SLEEPING THROUGH CLASS--WHEN YOU SHOW UP AT ALL, THAT IS. LYING TO YOUR AUNT MAY ABOUT YOUR JOB. SNEAKING OUT AT NIGHT.
DISAPPEARING WHEN SPIDER-MAN'S AROUND. SHOWING UP WITH BRUISES YOU WON'T EXPLAIN.
I KNOW WHAT'S GOING ON, PETER.
OH, GOD. HE KNOWS.

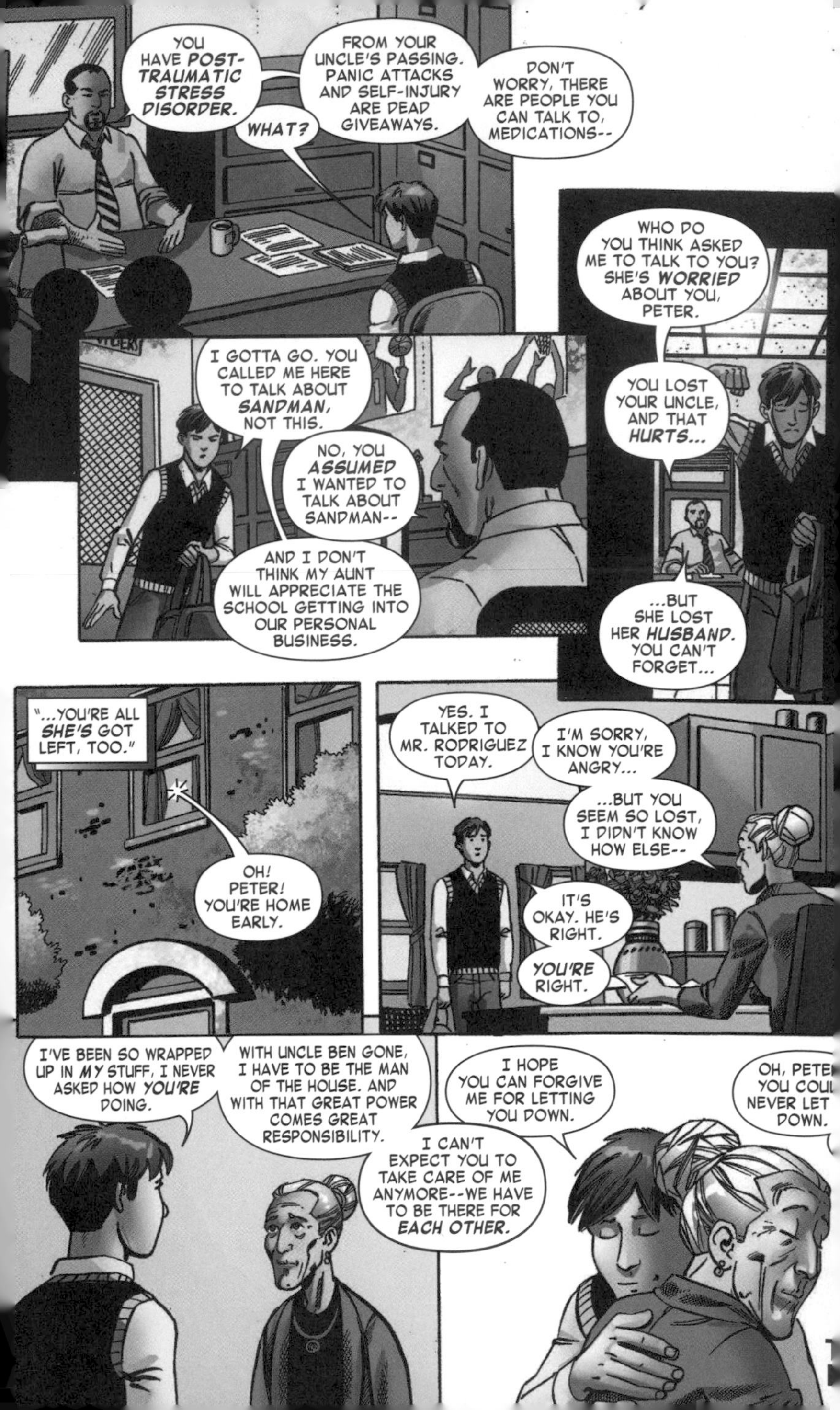
YOU HAVE POST-TRAUMATIC STRESS DISORDER.
WHAT?
FROM YOUR UNCLE'S PASSING. PANIC ATTACKS AND SELF-INJURY ARE DEAD GIVEAWAYS.
DON'T WORRY, THERE ARE PEOPLE YOU CAN TALK TO, MEDICATIONS--
I GOTTA GO. YOU CALLED ME HERE TO TALK ABOUT SANDMAN, NOT THIS.
NO, YOU ASSUMED I WANTED TO TALK ABOUT SANDMAN--
AND I DON'T THINK MY AUNT WILL APPRECIATE THE SCHOOL GETTING INTO OUR PERSONAL BUSINESS.
WHO DO YOU THINK ASKED ME TO TALK TO YOU? SHE'S WORRIED ABOUT YOU, PETER.
YOU LOST YOUR UNCLE, AND THAT HURTS...
...BUT SHE LOST HER HUSBAND. YOU CAN'T FORGET...
"...YOU'RE ALL SHE'S GOT LEFT, TOO."
OH! PETER! YOU'RE HOME EARLY.
YES. I TALKED TO MR. RODRIGUEZ TODAY.
I'M SORRY, I KNOW YOU'RE ANGRY...
...BUT YOU SEEM SO LOST, I DIDN'T KNOW HOW ELSE--
IT'S OKAY. HE'S RIGHT.
YOU'RE RIGHT.
I'VE BEEN SO WRAPPED UP IN MY STUFF, I NEVER ASKED HOW YOU'RE DOING.
WITH UNCLE BEN GONE, I HAVE TO BE THE MAN OF THE HOUSE. AND WITH THAT GREAT POWER COMES GREAT RESPONSIBILITY.
I CAN'T EXPECT YOU TO TAKE CARE OF ME ANYMORE--WE HAVE TO BE THERE FOR EACH OTHER.
I HOPE YOU CAN FORGIVE ME FOR LETTING YOU DOWN.